W9-BAG-452

2e

Instructor's Resource
Manual for Kaseberg's

Intermediate
Algebra
A Just-in-Time
Approach

Alice Kaseberg
Lane Community College

Laura Moore-Mueller
Green River Community College

Brooks/Cole
Thomson Learning

Australia · Canada · Mexico
Singapore · Spain · United Kingdom · United States

COPYRIGHT © 2000 by Brooks/Cole
A division of Thomson Learning
The Thomson Learning logo is a trademark used herein under license.

For more information about this or any other Brooks/Cole product, contact:
BROOKS/COLE
511 Forest Lodge Road
Pacific Grove, CA 93950 USA
www.brookscole.com
1-800-423-0563 (Thomson Learning Academic Resource Center)

For permission to use material from this work, contact us by
Web: www.thomsonrights.com
fax: 1-800-730-2215
phone: 1-800-730-2214

Printed in the United States of America

5   4   3   2   1

ISBN 0-534-37348-8

Contents

PREFACE

Introducing your "workshop in a notebook" —it's almost as good as spending a day with Alice Kaseberg, author of Introductory Algebra: A Just-in-Time Approach.

Thriving with Change

Change is like riding a bicycle—at first you fall off, then you fly! Some new wrinkles for the old algebra curriculum and the beginnings of a teaching style make-over for you. New century, new demands. Testing the waters before you dive in. It's extra time well spent!

Get Your Colleagues on Board

Here are some tips on how to help your support staff help you. Filling in the support staff so they can steer your students straight. Finding ready-made applications problems from colleagues in other departments.

Expectations: You and Your Students

New wrinkles and a new teaching style means a few new expectations. For your students, life skills and algebra they can use. For you, new ways to help the students help themselves and a three-fold approach to meet their needs.

INTRODUCTION TO DEVELOPMENTAL ALGEBRA AND THE *JUST-IN-TIME* APPROACH

You get the inside story on how Kaseberg uses her textbook week by week, and how to start your teaching-style make-over. Here you'll find overall course plans depending on your school's schedule and your students' needs.

Course Planning

Your students' success depends on how you plan the course. Don't miss Kaseberg's tips on how to facilitate student success in independent-study courses.

Week-by-Week Course Plans

These quick-reference charts give you suggested plans for ten-, fifteen-week courses.

Strategies for Teaching and Learning

This is the heart of Kaseberg's Just-in-Time approach. Learn the "whys and wherefores" of these powerful teaching and learning strategies, then your make-over will happen naturally. And it will be fun!

TIPS ON CLASSROOM MANAGEMENT

How to get the most out of every class session. Here is the voice of Kaseberg's experience!

SECTION LESSONS

Here is a set of pre-packaged lesson plans—one for each section in the textbook. You can use each lesson as is, or pick and choose whatever is useful to you.

Each section lesson has information you will need as you prepare for class, followed by a complete lesson, overhead transparency masters you may need. Some section lessons also include worksheets for group activities.

Expressions and Equations
Equations, Functions, and Linear Functions
Quadratic Functions: Applications and Solutions to Equations

STUDENT'S SOLUTIONS MANUAL

PREFACE

During the past five years, Alice Kaseberg has given numerous workshops addressing the most commonly asked questions about her textbook *Intermediate Algebra: A Just-in-Time Approach*. This *Instructor's Resource Manual* (IRM) is intended to be your personal "workshop in a notebook." The first part of this resource manual gives the overview of Kaseberg's approach to developmental-algebra instruction that you would get in a workshop. The Section Lessons, in the second part, provide the day-to-day details that will help you implement Kaseberg's approach. This resource manual is designed to make it as easy as possible for you make the transition from the traditional lecture format to a teaching style that allows for students to actively participate in the learning process.

Thriving with Change

The introductory material that follows is intended show you the "big picture" that you would see in one of Kaseberg's workshops. Whether you are an experienced teacher or new to the profession, changing your instructional style takes commitment and effort. The more thorough your command of Kaseberg's approach and why she uses it, the more success you and your students will enjoy.

What's the Difference?

The mathematics curriculum in *Intermediate Algebra: A Just-in-Time Approach* is standard for developmental-algebra courses; though, as the title implies, the order in which the topics are presented varies at times from the standard curriculum.

In Kaseberg's approach, the main difference from other developmental-algebra courses is *how* the lessons are presented. Kaseberg's material suggests a unique interaction between the students, the instructor, and the mathematics. Many of the lessons use guided discovery and problem solving as powerful teaching tools. With this approach, you act in the role of "guide and fellow traveler," who shows the students how to find and unlock the secrets of mathematics for themselves. What a relief and delight that you can

The world is changing around us and, if we don't change, we may find ourselves and our students left behind.

shed the guise of the all-knowing mathematician and join the students as they explore and master the mathematics in their world!

Why Change?

While it is possible to use Kaseberg's material in a traditional instruction mode, it would be a shame to waste the potential of this rich approach. You may say to yourself, "We have always taught mathematics the way we were taught, why should we change?" The answer is simple: The world is changing around us and, if we don't change, we may find ourselves and our students left behind. As told in this anecdote by British author J. E. Gordon in *Structures or Why Things Don't Fall Down*, (Penguin Books, New York 1978), consider what happened 150 years ago to the embarrassed British sailmakers, who had failed to change with the times:

> [S]ailmaking has been an important industry ever since the beginning of history, [however, certain] elementary facts about canvas never fully dawned upon European sailmakers.
>
> Rational modern sailmaking began in the United States early in the nineteenth century. Although the consequence [of the new approach to sailmaking] was that American ships could frequently sail faster . . . than British ones, it required something like an earthquake to bring the facts home to English sailmakers. This was provided by the publicity associated with the schooner yacht America, which came over . . . in 1851 to compete with the fastest English yachts . . . in a race around the Isle of Wight.
>
> When the Queen was told that the America was the first yacht to have crossed the finishing line, she asked 'And who is second?'
>
> 'There is no second in sight yet, Your Majesty.'

As educators, let us hope we can adapt to a new role in the classroom more readily than the 19th century British sailmakers were able to change their ways.

Start Gradually

If you choose to dive right in with Kaseberg's approach, the Section Lessons in this Instructor's Resource Manual provide you with a detailed lesson for every Section in the textbook. The Section Lessons suggest what to do and even what to say.

On the other hand, it may be wise to start out gradually, staying within your comfort zone as you gain skill and confidence in guided discovery and its effectiveness. Changing everything all at once can make it difficult to judge what works for you and what does not. Furthermore, if you are uneasy with the lesson, your students will be uneasy.

If you choose to gradually incorporate guided discovery and problem solving into your current teaching style, you might look to the Section Lessons for ideas on how to make guided discovery work for you. Start with one element from a Lesson; for example, have the students do the Warm-up and discuss their homework in groups (which is the first recommended activity for most Section Lessons), then proceed with a lesson format you are familiar with. As you begin to see how successful and enthusiastic the students are about working together in a discovery mode, you may want to use more class time for the group activities suggested in the Section Lessons. Use this manual in the way that best suits your needs—as an occasional quick reference to supplement the text, as a guide to setting homework assignments, or as a major component for day-to-day planning.

Preparation Time

Kaseberg's nontraditional approach to teaching algebra will work only if you, the instructor, are prepared: List the examples you want to present in class and the points you want to stress. Plan to use the Warm-up exercises to reinforce, review, or anticipate concepts in the lesson. Decide what might be done in small groups and what is best covered in a whole-class discussion. Plan the coaching you want to do on the homework exercises. Find relevant applications and related topics that may be of interest to your students in their other courses. Be prepared before class with any special equipment or materials you want to use.

Each Section Lesson in this manual has been prepared by an instructor experienced in using *Intermediate Algebra: A Just-in-Time Approach* and contains the preparation elements suggested above. Even with the aid of this *Instructor's Resource Manual*, teaching from Kaseberg's textbook is not a five-minute prep. Though the topics and concepts are part of the standard developmental-algebra curriculum, some of the material in the textbook might be new to you. Allow yourself enough preparation time to learn some new things, and be prepared to have some fun!

Get Your Colleagues on Board

No matter how enthusiastic you may be about using *Intermediate Algebra: A Just-in-Time Approach*, it may be new to your department colleagues, your support team, and the faculty in other departments. The more information about your course that your colleagues have, the easier it may be for them to support you.

Advisors and Counselors

Getting your support team behind you is the most valuable effort you can make. Chances are good that a course based on Kaseberg's approach will be different from the mathematics courses that your college's advisors, counselors and placement-test office staff took when they were in school. If you have anything in your course that is different from the algebra courses usually taught at your school—from graphing calculators to group instruction, or portfolios to discovery learning—be sure to explain these differences and your motivation behind them to your support team.

Make sure your support team has accurate information about your course including the name of someone in your department who can answer their questions. Getting them on board means they can explain your course to students who may question your approach.

Other Departments

Ask faculty from other departments to provide you with common formulas or math problems from in their courses. Using these problems in class adds relevance for the students and authenticity to your curriculum.

Expectations: You and Your Students

This type of course may be as new to your students as it is to you. The more you set the stage for your students to take responsibility for their own learning, the more you will learn.

What Students Can Expect

This may be the first algebra class taught in this style that many of your students have taken, but it won't be their first math class. Therefore, the students come to you with preconceived notions of how math is taught, and that notion most likely includes a traditional view of algebra instruction. You may have to sell the students on what you are offering in this course:

Algebra that students can use. The course gives students experience with math problems they will encounter in their other courses. Many of the applications settings in the textbook have been drawn directly from materials for other programs, such as food services, business, chemistry, engineering, and health care.

A solid foundation. Kaseberg's developmental algebra provides a solid foundation for further college-level mathematics courses.

Algebra that students can relate to. Kaseberg's materials draw on the mathematics in students' daily lives. For example, students learn that inequalities, far from being an arcane mathematics device, is the basis for calculating your body-mass index, and that a bounded region describes how many people you can invite to a party on a limited budget.

Skills for the workplace. Figuring out how to use available resources, locating information, sharing information, and working cooperatively with others or in teams are common skills required for success in today's work place. The explorations, projects, and group work recommended throughout this course provide opportunities to develop all of these skills. It further empowers students to think through a problem and to benefit

...the best way to learn and remember something is to immediately teach it to someone else.

from and appreciate different points of view about how to approach a problem.

What You Can Expect: Students Learn by Teaching

In *The 7 Habits of Highly Effective People* (Fireside, 1990), author Stephen Covey reminds us that the best way to learn and remember something is to immediately teach it to someone else. Working in groups gives students the opportunity to learn by teaching.

It is safe to say that many of your students will be unfamiliar with working in a cooperative, non-competitive academic setting. However, it won't take them long to see the benefits of working in a group when they put their heads together to complete Exercises 1 to 18 in Section 1.0. The exercises call for the students to match words with definitions and clearly show the students how a group has more information than an individual.

What You Can Expect: Student Learning Styles

Because your students have different cultural backgrounds and a wide variety of past and present life experiences, no single example or presentation of a topic in mathematics will make sense to every student. Consider the different ways people learn directions to a friend's house. Depending on the person's leaning style they can quickly learn directions that are given in words with a list of intersections and turns (verbally), drawn on a map (visually), or from having been there before with someone else (kinesthetically).

Algebra students may learn better from words (a verbal approach); drawings, pictures, and graphs (a visual approach); getting up and moving around or working with a physical model (a kinesthetic approach); or a combination of these approaches. To be successful, students need the opportunity to have mathematics presented in a way that suits their learning styles. In the long run, it is advantageous for students to try learning in a variety of styles.

Addressing the needs of all learners—verbal, visual, or kinesthetic—is a high priority in mathematics education. To help students achieve success in algebra, *Intermediate Algebra: A Just-in-Time Approach* uses a threefold approach to lesson presentations to fit student's varied learning styles. To do this, Kaseberg has included as many alternative models to each concept as space permits. The threefold models are numeric using words and symbols for verbal learners, graphic using tables and graphs for visual learner, and physical using objects and drawings for kinesthetic learners. The Section Lessons in this *Instructor's Resource Manual* are intended to help you incorporate these different approaches in your classroom presentations.

What You Can Expect: Patience from the Students

If you had to order shoes for every student in your class, the last thing they would want is one size and style for everyone. Yet students come to class expecting one style of traditional teaching, and often need reminders to appreciate the variety of learning styles among their classmates.

The verbal and visual learning styles are readily accommodated in a classroom setting, where a chalkboard or overhead projector and an abundance of words are always on hand. However, kinesthetic learners need manipulatives, body movements, and real-world images. For example, cardboard squares and rectangles might be used to model x^2 and xy in polynomials; cards might be dealt out to demonstrate the distributive property; hugs might be used to represent parentheses in the associative property; and commuting from home to school might be invoked to illustrate the commutative property.

Remind the students that although some ways of doing algebra may not make sense to them, these methods will help someone else. Let them know that you expect them to be patient during lessons that suit their other classmates' learning styles.   ●

INTRODUCTION

DEVELOPMENTAL-ALGEBRA INSTRUCTION
A *JUST-IN-TIME* APPROACH

Course Planning

You may be new to teaching a course using *Intermediate Algebra: A Just-in-Time Approach*, new to teaching altogether, or you may be an experienced teacher looking for new ways to accomplish familiar tasks. Whatever your background, it is a challenge to accomplish your goals for an introductory algebra course and address the varied needs of all your students.

As a developmental-algebra instructor, you are sure to encounter students with a variety of experiences with algebra—some students have taken intermediate algebra and are just reviewing, others have taken algebra at this level and were not successful, and still others have never studied intermediate algebra. The following ideas and suggestions may help you to plan your course and adopt teaching strategies that will help you meet your students' needs.

Structuring the Course

The core sections of *Intermediate Algebra: A Just-in-Time Approach* and the suggested course structures which begin on page 3 are designed for forty lessons of forty-five to fifty minutes. The author assumes that students in the course have passed a placement test on introductory algebra or completed either a ten-week review of beginning algebra or a fifteen-week introduction to algebra. To accommodate the varieties of prior algebra experience, consider the course options listed below.

For remedial students and those weak in algebra—

- In a ten-week quarter system with classes that meet four times a week: Omit Sections 3.5, 4.2, 4.4, Chapter 7, and Sections 8.2 through 8.6.

- In a fifteen-week semester system with classes that meet four times a week: Omit Sections 4.2, 4.4, 7.4, 7.5, 8.4, 8.5, and 8.6.

For students with successful experience in algebra—

- In a ten week quarter system with classes that meet four times a week: Omit Sections 3.5, 4.2, 4.4, 5.5, 6.3, 7.5, and 8.2 through 8.6.

- In a fifteen-week semester system with classes that meet four times a week: Do one section per day; choose selectively from Chapter 1 to complete it during the first week.

Note: In this course plan we are still on quadratic functions in Week Six, but students have used the calculator for graphing and regression (to fit linear and quadratic equations); and they have intuitively solved systems of equations by solving equations with graphs (linear and nonlinear). Also, students have the foundation for identifying linear, quadratic, and exponential functions with differences in sequences; and they have worked with square roots and imaginary numbers.

This plan omits inequalities (1.4, 3.5, 8.6), shifts in graphs (4.2, half of 7.1), inverse variation (5.2), polynomial long division (5.5), addition, subtraction, and rationalization of radicals (6.3), the natural numbers (7.5), matrices (8.2, 8.3), conic sections and nonlinear systems (8.4, 8.5).

Gaining Extra Time

There are a few things you can do to gain some extra class time throughout the term, especially if you plan ahead.

Combine section lessons and test days—The suggested course plans (see IRM pages 5 and 6) include recommendations to start certain new sections on the same day as reviewing for a test. In these sections, the topics can be summarized briefly the day before the test with the homework not due until the day after the test.

These sections provide productive work for days normally lost in the term's schedule and keep students in a work-on-mathematics-every-day rhythm. If your students tend to forget a delayed homework assignment, try giving them two take-home questions as part the test and write a reminder of the homework on the take-home test paper.

Eliminate in-class tests—If possible, arrange for a supervisor to monitor students so they can take tests and quizzes outside of the regular class period.

Planning Independent-Study Courses

At orientation, remind the students that independent-study courses are harder to complete than lecture courses. They will have a good chance at success if they follow your suggestions on attendance, peer teaching, and reading strategies.

Facilitate regular attendance—Schools should schedule regular times for independent-study students to meet with instructors or tutors, and students should commit to a regularly scheduled time for their independent-study course. Stress attendance and the need for regular study. If the independent-study lab cannot require attendance for the entire course, then perhaps there is a way to require it for the first two weeks to give students a good start. Have students report in by sending an e-mail summary of their work.

Facilitate peer teaching—Help students get acquainted with each other and encourage them to form their own study groups. Students have more perseverance if they work together.

In the laboratory setting, provide well-marked study tables for each course taught. Encourage students taking the same course to sit together. Keep a limited range of courses in any given lab/study area to reduce intimidation.

On orientation day, have students in the same course participate together in an activity, such as taking a group quiz over the orientation material, instead of listening to someone read the syllabus content. On the second day, have students discuss their results from Section 1.0, Exercises 1 to 9. After their discussion of these exercises, point out how their discussion is typical of many mathematics topics they will encounter in this

> **Students have more perseverance if they work together.**

course: Some students will ask questions and some students will provide hints, strategies, or ways of thinking about answers. Because of a variety of mathematics backgrounds and language skills, the teacher and learner roles students play will change from one topic to the next.

Stress the use of reading strategies—Students who use effective reading strategies will enjoy greater success in the course. Provide students with a large 4-inch by 6-inch bookmark printed with the strategies listed below. Stress the importance of using the strategies consistently.

Coach the students to use the following reading strategies:

- Do the warm-ups at the beginning of each section. These exercises review or introduce skill and concepts covered in the section. Introduce skills or concepts covered in the section.

- Read the paragraphs preceding an example. You should not expect to fully understand everything you read the first time; so plan to read and reread the material two more times before trying to work the examples.

- Read the problem given in the example. Then cover up the solution while you work the problem. Then study the solution given in the text. (Attempting to work the examples helps the students relate the given problem to material they have just read. The work also encourages a more careful reading of the problem and the solution.) ●

SLOWER-PACED COURSES

TEN-WEEK QUARTER WITH CLASSES MEETING FOUR HOURS A WEEK

Week	Sections	Week's Focus
Week One	1.0, 1.1, 1.2, 1.3	Review, Tables, Graphs, and Graphing Calculator
Week Two	1.4, 2.0, 2.1	Functions and Linear Equations
Week Three	2.2, 2.3, 2.4/Review, Test 1	Build and Identify Linear Equations
Week Four	3.0, 3.1, 3.2, 3.3	Factoring, Square Roots, Quadratic Equations
Week Five	3.4, 4.0, 4.1	Solving Quadratic Equations, Special Products, Modeling
Week Six	4.3, 4.5, 4.5/Review, Test 2	Complex Numbers, Minimum/Maximum
Week Seven	5.0, 5.1, 5.3 5.4	Unit Analysis, Proportions, Rational Expressions Rational Expressions
Week Eight	5.5, 5.6, 6.0, 6.1	Division of Polynomials, Solving Rational Equations, Exponents and Scientific Notation, Rational Exponents
Week Nine	6.2, 6.3, 6.4	Exponents, Radicals, Inverse Functions, and Solving Power and Root Equations
Week Ten	Test, 8.0, 8.1, Review	Systems of Equations

FIFTEEN-WEEK QUARTER WITH CLASSES MEETING FOUR HOURS A WEEK

Week	Sections	Week's Focus
Week One	1.0, 1.1, 1.2, 1.3	Review Tables, Graphs, and Graphing Calculator
Week Two	1.4, 2.0, 2.1	Inequalities, Functions, Linear Equations
Week Three	2.2, 2.3, 2.4/Review, Test 1	Build and Identify Linear Equations
Week Four	3.0, 3.1, 3.2, 3.3	Factoring, Square Roots, Quadratic Equations
Week Five	3.4, 3.4, 3.5, 4.0	Solving Quadratic Equations, Inequalities, Special Products
Week Six	4.1, 4.3, 4.5, 4.5/Review	Modeling, Complex Numbers, Minimum/Maximum
Week Seven	Test 2, 5.0, 5.1, 5.2	Unit Analysis, Proportions
Week Eight	5.3, 5.4, 5.5	Rational Expressions and Operations, Division of Polynomials
Week Nine	5.6, 6.0, 6.1	Solving Rational Equations, Exponents and Scientific Notation, Rational Exponents
Week Ten	6.3, 6.3, 6.4, Test 3	Radicals, Inverse Functions, and Solving Power and Root Equations
Week Eleven	7.0, 7.1, 7.2	Exponential Equations, Logarithms and Logarithmic Functions
Week Twelve	7.2, 7.3	Logarithmic Equations, Applications
Week Thirteen	8.0, 8.1, Test 4	Systems of Equations
Week Fourteen	8.2, 8.3	Solving Systems of Equations with Matrices
Week Fifteen	Final Exam	

AVERAGE-PACED COURSES

TEN-WEEK QUARTER WITH CLASSES MEETING FOUR HOURS A WEEK

Week	Sections	Week's Focus
Week One	1.0, 1.1, 1.2, 1.3, 1.4	Review, Tables, Graphs, and Graphing Calculator
Week Two	1.4, 2.0, 2.1	Functions and Linear Equations
Week Three	2.2, 2.3, 2.4/Review, Test 1	Build and Identify Linear Equations
Week Four	3.0, 3.1, 3.2, 3.3	Factoring, Square Roots, Quadratic Equations
Week Five	3.4, 4.0, 4.1, 4.3	Solving Quadratic Equations, Special Products, Modeling, Complex Numbers
Week Six	4.5, 5.0, 5.1, 5.2, 5.3	Unit Analysis, Proportions, Rational Expressions
Week Seven	5.3, 5.4, 5.6	Rational Expressions
Week Eight	Test 2/6.0, 6.15.5, 5.6, 6.0, 6.1	Exponents, Radicals, Exponential Functions
Week Nine	6.2, 6.3, 6.4	Exponential Functions, Logarithmic Functions
Week Ten	Test, 8.0, 8.1, Review	Properties of Logarithms, Systems of Equations

FIFTEEN-WEEK QUARTER WITH CLASSES MEETING FOUR HOURS A WEEK

Week	Sections	Week's Focus
Week One	1.0, 1.1, 1.2, 1.3, 1.4	Review Tables, Graphs, Inequalities, Graphing Calculator
Week Two	2.0, 2.1/Quiz 2, 2.2	Functions, Linear Equations
Week Three	2.2, 2.3, 2.4/Review, Test 1	Build and Identify Linear Equations
Week Four	3.0, 3.1, 3.2, 3.3	Factoring, Square Roots, Quadratic Equations
Week Five	3.4, 3.5, 4.0, 4., 4.2	Solving Quadratic Equations, Inequalities, Special Products
Week Six	4.3, 4.5, 4.5/Review, Test 2	Modeling, Complex Numbers, Completing the Square, Minimum/Maximum
Week Seven	5.0, 5.1, 5.2, 5.3	Unit Analysis, Proportions, Rational Expressions
Week Eight	5.4, 5.5, 5.6, 6.0	Rational Expressions and Equations, Division of Polynomials, Exponents and Scientific Notation
Week Nine	6.1, 6.3, 6.3, 6.4	Rational Exponents, Solving Power and Root Equations
Week Ten	Test 3, 7.0, 7.1, 7.2	Radicals, Inverse Functions, and Solving Power and Root Equations
Week Eleven	7.2, 7.3, .4	Exponential Equations, Logarithms Equations
Week Twelve	Test 4, 7.5, 8.0, 8.1	Natural Numbers, Systems of Equations
Week Thirteen	8.2, 8.3	Solving Systems of Equations with Matrices
Week Fourteen	8.4, 8.5, 8.6	Conic Sections, Solving Systems Equations and Inequalities
Week Fifteen	Final Exam	

Strategies for Teaching and Learning

Each section lesson in this *Instructor's Resource Manual* incorporates the teaching strategies discussed here. The more familiar you are with the strategies and the ideas behind them, the more success and satisfaction you will get from implementing them.

Problem Solving

The term problem solving as it is used in *Intermediate Algebra: A Just-in-Time Approach* refers both to strategies for solving problems and asking questions.

Problem-solving steps and strategies—George Polya's four-step approach to problem solving—understand the problem, make a plan to solve the problem, carry out the plan, and check the solution—is introduced in Section 1.1 and revisited where appropriate. After introducing the four steps, the text focuses on planning strategies.

Section 1.1 introduces the strategies of *looking for a number pattern, making a table of inputs and outputs, and using manipulatives.* The strategy of finding number patterns continues in Sections 2.4, 3.2, 4.1 and 7.0. *Making a graph* as a strategy for solving problems first appears in Section 1.2. *Working backwards* is the fundamental idea in solving equations and formulas in Section 1.3. *Choosing a test number* or ordered pair and checking it is used for drawing a line graphs and identifying half-planes for two-variable inequalities in Section 1.4 and solving systems of inequalities in Sections 8.6. *Making a systematic list* is an essential component of factoring in Section 3.0. *Guessing and checking*, which is a natural extension of choosing a test number for inequalities, is essential in building and solving systems of equations in Section 8.0.

What are problem-solving questions?—A good problem-solving question may have more than one correct answer and cannot be answered from rote memory. There is often more than one right way to go about solving the problem.

The term problem solving is frequently misused interchangeably with the term *word problem*. Here is a pair of rudimentary questions that illustrate the difference:

Word problem. Jack and Jill have ten graphing calculators between them. Jill has eight graphing calculators, how many does Jack have?

Problem-solving question. Jack and Jill have ten graphing calculators between them. Jill has more calculators than Jack. What are the possible combinations of calculators between them?

To solve the word problem, the student can use the problem-solving steps of understand, plan, carry out, and check. However, the word problem may be solved more quickly from rote memory. On the other hand, even though the problem-solving form of the question may be solved mentally, it requires a moment of thought using guess and check and eliminating possibilities—two powerful problem-solving strategies.

Student reactions to problem solving—Over the years, instructors have noticed varying student reactions to problem-solving. Some students are disconcerted at first when they can't immediately come up with the answer to a question. It is often a struggle for them to accept that some answers can only by found by exploration and discovery—problem solving—rather than from rote memory. These students may balk at this approach at first. You can assure these students that in the long run they will know more because they won't have to hold everything in memory.

On the other hand, students who have been less successful in the traditional lecture setting are often delighted to find out they don't need to know everything "off the top of their head" and that strategies they've often devised covertly have *names* and are legitimate approaches to solving problems! These students are further encouraged as they become armed with more strategies for mastering the mysteries of mathematics.

Discovery Learning

Many textbooks simply state facts, such as principles, definitions, and properties, then give examples. In discovery learning, an exploration is provided, followed by questions, summaries, and examples. The goal is for students to learn to identify patterns and relationships and to draw their own conclusions. Well designed explorations lead to the correct conclusions.

Discovery takes faith in the student and patience on the part of the instructor. Discovery requires that the student take responsibility for learning. Discovery implies that the teacher gives up being the authority and source of all knowledge.

Not every algebra concept or skill lends itself to discovery learning. For example, students can accurately derive the many number properties by examining examples of the properties in action. However, it is more effective to use a conventional "show-and-tell" format to introduce the steps for solving formulas.

The Threefold Approach

Depending on the content of the lesson, *Intermediate Algebra: A Just-in-Time Approach* and the Section Lessons in this manual vary the presentation modes of questions (requiring problem solving or rote responses) and concepts (using discovery or show-and-tell). Regardless of which mode of presentation is used for questions and concepts, Kaseberg uses the threefold models—numeric, graphic, and physical—as much as possible to allow students to access the information according to their individual learning styles.

Vocabulary

Learning the vocabulary in the language of mathematics is one of the most overlooked areas of difficulty for math students. The meaning of a word as it is used in math often differs from its everyday usage. Consider the different meanings of such words as term, factor, rational, irrational, and real. Many math words are strange to students, for example, quotient, denominator, distributive, and vertex.

Point out how to locate where words are defined in the textbook. (Definitions appear in boxes or in text with the words printed in bold-face and the definition in italics.) Call the students' attention to the vocabulary lists given at the end of each chapter. Remind them to use the Glossary/Index, where the words in chapter vocabulary lists are defined and page numbers are given for locating where the words are introduced in the text. Repeat important words during your presentation of the material to help your students learn the vocabulary in context. Remember that students appreciate hearing why a word was chosen to name a concept and what the different parts of a word mean.

Student confusion over the meaning of the word solution—Note that we use "solution" before the answers to each example. Yet, we use the word "solve" only when describing the steps for solving equations. We use "simplify" to describe operations with expressions, and "evaluate" when referring to placing numbers or expressions into equations, formulas, or expressions. No wonder students get confused! To help them keep this vocabulary straight, on the inside front cover of the textbook, we have included a list of these words and how we use them.

Planning Assignments

Give assignments several days in advance or for the full term (you will find a recommended homework assignment included with every Section Lesson in this manual). Adult students may be employed or have family obligations that make it difficult for them to allocate exactly the same amount of time each day to work on assignments. Thus, it is important to give them the lead time they need to fit the homework into their schedules.

Each exercise in *Intermediate Algebra: A Just-in-time Approach* has been thoughtfully written based on the textbook's pedagogy. Do every homework assignment yourself! This will make the homework a shared experience with your students and better prepare you for their questions. When you do the homework exercises yourself, you may find some delightful surprises.

Build activities into the assignments that require students to read the next day's material or review a skill or concept needed to understand the next day's lesson. This improves student performance and makes your job easier.

> **When you do the homework exercises yourself, you may find some delightful surprises.**

Applications

You may find it convenient to skip some applications. Remind students which applications are important to you so they can read selectively. This may be particularly helpful for the English as a Second Language (ESL) student.

Projects

You will find an Index of Projects on page 685 of the textbook. During the first term you use the textbook, plan to use one or two projects as in-class activities. Projects marked with an asterisk are specially designed for small groups, inside or outside class. If you are already using projects in your classes, the projects in *Intermediate Algebra: A Just-in-Time Approach* may provide a source of new ideas for you.

In your second term using the textbook, include projects in your syllabus. One approach to projects is to require students to do three projects of their choice, due on three specific dates. You might list four additional projects for the students to choose from to do for an extra-credit project.

To avoid last-minute efforts at the end of the term, it is recommended that projects be submitted one week after the section is covered in class (or a week after the homework for that section is due). Specific deadlines permit you to return the projects in a timely manner and give rave reviews of any impressive projects. If none are impressive, then be specific about the quality of work you want. Give students feedback and let them improve their scores with more work within a limited time period. The projects might be awarded points or might be part of a portfolio.

Activities with CBR and CBL

The manuals that accompany the Texas Instruments Calculator-Based Ranger (CBR), and the older but more flexible Calculator-Based Laboratory (CBL) have instructions for a number of activities. The table below lists experiments suggested in the manual that are appropriate to this course (refer to the manuals for details).

The CBL requires programs, which are listed in the manual or are available by linking through the Texas Instruments website at www.ti.com/calc. All of the activities require at least a TI-82 or a TI-83 calculator and linking cable.

Tests

Most developmental-algebra students have had a negative experience with mathematics and especially with tests. Offer study suggestions, think about the test environment, and consider alternative evaluation and assessment strategies.

Study suggestions—To prepare for tests, students should write important facts, vocabulary, and concepts on 3- by 5-inch index cards or on notebook pages. The cards, a review of homework papers, and sample exercises provide the basis for studying for a test.

Test environment—Students are tense during test taking, so make the environment as friendly as possible. Place an easy question at the beginning of the test or tell students what the first question will be. Explain that it is important to keep the room as quiet as possible and then request that students not leave early. Ask students to go over their tests to check for careless errors and to bring something to read or to work on after they finish the test. If someone must leave early, arrange for a different testing location or ask them to sit by the door and zip their backpack or carry bag outside the room after they leave. Mention the no-leaving-early policy on the first day of class and again each day for a week before the test. Stress the aspect of courtesy to fellow students. Few students want to be intentionally rude.

Testing and Assessment Strategies

Instructors have a variety of ways to deal with tests, make-up tests, and re-takes. Variations on

---

ACTIVITIES FROM MANUALS FOR TEXAS INSTRUMENTS CBR AND CBL CALCULATORS

MATH TOPIC	EQUIPMENT	ACTIVITY
Linear Functions	CBR	Activity 1, Match the Graph
Linear Functions	CBR	Activity 2, Toy Car
Quadratic Functions	CBR	Activity 4, Bouncing Ball
Quadratic Functions	CBR	Activity 5, Rolling Ball
Functions and Slope	CBL, motion detector	M1, Take a Hike
Quadratic Equations	CBL, motion detector	M2, What Goes Up Must Come Down
Exponential Functions	CBL, temperature probe	M5, Coffee to Go
Inverse Square Variation	CBL, light probe	M6, Light Intensity
Geometric Sequence or Exponential Function	CBL, motion detector	P2, Rebound Height

modes of testing include: untimed tests, take-home tests, group tests, and two day tests with feedback where students complete the test on day one and come back the next day to re-work missed problems for a portion of the original credit. Some instructors give the re-work as a take-home. Some instructors give multiple tests during a term and count only a portion of them for the grade. Other instructors allow the students to retake one test (within a week of the original test). Another variation is to have the last day of the term be for make-up tests, in which students may take another form of one of their prior tests.

Some instructors allow notes on tests. Other instructors have students prepare a personal reference manual without specific examples and then allow students access to the manual on their final exam. This manual can be the basis for a mathematics reference guide to be continued in other courses.

A number of instructors point out that using sources appropriately is a learned skill and therefore give open book tests. Even the national Fundamentals of Engineering examinations for entry into the professional engineering field are open book. Students bring stacks of engineering books and notes to the exam. The tests are known for challenging the students' problem-solving skills, but the open-book format does not penalize students for forgetting a formula.

Think about separating skill tests from problem-solving tests. Many colleges are defining a set of essential skills and requiring that students pass gateway or skill tests at an 80% or 90% level.

Make-up tests—When testing facilities are limited, students might take the first try in class and subsequent tries during a particular hour each week.

Grading tests—In grading tests (and homework, when possible), give students feedback on their concept understanding, procedural mastery, use of problem solving, and communication skills.

Learning from Tests

Students may not make effective use of their tests as a learning tool. Require re-works of tests

The graphing calculator is a magnificent tool, but it does not replace understanding.

whether or not you give any credit. If you go over a test in class, afterwards, you might ask students to write a sentence about what they did wrong on each problem, rework the problem, and then write a sentence describing the correct procedure.

Quizzes

Think carefully about your purpose in giving quizzes. If the purpose is to encourage students to keep up on the material by attending class and doing assignments, then perhaps homework quizzes may be useful. On homework quizzes students are given questions from homework exercises. This reduces stress because the student who has done all the homework knows what questions to expect. If the purpose of the quiz is to check skills, then consider gateway tests.

Portfolios

A portfolio is a collection of work that contains the student's self-assessment of what has been learned from the course and documents his/her work. One effective assessment procedure includes a combination of portfolios and skills testing. See American Mathematical Association of Two-Year Colleges (AMATYC)[1] and National Council of Mathematics (NCTM)[2] publications for a variety of ideas on using portfolios.

Graphing Calculators

Intermediate Algebra: A Just-in-Time Approach assumes that students will be required to use a graphing calculator. The graphing calculator is a magnificent tool, but it does not replace understanding.

Students may use a graphing calculator to evaluate expressions, verify the equivalence of algebraic statements for a given input, solve equations, solve systems of linear equations, graph, find the equation of a line given two points, fit an equation to data, and more. However, before students can use this tool effectively, they must understand the meaning of expressions, the meaning of evaluation of expressions, the reading of tables and graphs, the meaning of equations, the interpretation of slopes and intercepts, the

---

[1] Visit http://www.amatyc.org for information on AMATYC publications.
[2] Visit http://www.nctm.org for information on NCTM publications.

meaning of intersections of equations, and so forth. The calculator does not replace understanding.

To reduce a proliferation of inappropriate calculators being brought to class, include a note in your school's class schedule specifying the model of graphing calculator you will be using for classroom demonstrations.

Tips on Classroom Management

The following tips on using the Instructor's Resource Manual reflect accumulated experience of instructors with some years of experience using the First Editions of Introductory and Intermediate Algebra: A Just-in-Time Approach. Each of these instructors has their own style of teaching and unique departmental circumstances. A standard format for the lessons has been used to help you find the information you need, but the lessons themselves may vary in approach depending on the style of the instructor who wrote it.

Be Prepared!

Most of the suggestions below will work only if you, the instructor, are prepared. It bears repeating: Work assigned exercises yourself. Also work the examples and study their solutions. The Section Lessons provide you with specific suggestions for the following tasks as you prepare your classroom presentation:

- List examples you want to present and ideas you want students to learn.
- Select warm-up problems that reinforce, review, or anticipate.
- Decide what might be best done in small groups, full-group discussion, or by lecture.
- Plan the suggestions you want to make about the homework exercises.
- Prepare any special equipment you want to use.

Little things make a difference—If ecologically or financially feasible, use paper of one particular color for all material for your course. This will help students identify and organize material for your course. Have every handout, quiz or test three-hole punched.

Post the agenda before class—As indicated earlier, it is not an easy task to address the needs of all your students and accomplish your goals for each class. To make the most of every minute, write your objectives and agenda on the board. This will get the class underway as soon as students enter the room. Students will also get in the habit of arriving to class on time to avoid missing anything. Here's a sample of objectives and an agenda: "Today we will discuss the rectangular coordinate graph, how it determines positions on a flat surface, and how it displays our

---

Getting Acquainted

Your full name:_____Name you go by: _____

Telephone number:_____Your Major:_____

Highest math class completed in high school:_____

Last math class taken and when:_____

Highest math you can do on a calculator:_____

A personal goal, hobby, or area of interest:_____

_____

Number of credit hours you are taking this term:_____

Number of hours you work each week:_____

---

input-output information." Then outline how you will use the class time, for example, "Warm-up: 5 minutes, Questions on Homework: 10 minutes," and so on. You will find suggested lesson formats with each Section Lesson below. Refer to the agenda at the end of the class to bring closure to the lesson.

Start Each Class with a Warm-up

Write warm-up problems on the board, or note warm-ups from the text that students should complete. Warm-up problems should take five minutes total and include problems that review prior work, highlight prior test problems, or cover prerequisite skills for some portion of the in-class activity or lecture. Warm-ups ensure that a focused review of concepts occurs at the beginning of class rather than in the middle of the discussion or presentation of new material.

Some instructors prefer to lead into the lecture or activity with an oral warm-up question. This approach has the disadvantage of involving only a few students. A written warm-up or lead-in question involves all students, regardless of ease with which they speak up in class.

Written warm-ups ensure that students take an active role in the class immediately upon entering the room. Have the students compare their answers to warm-ups, which encourages communication—

an important prerequisite to working effectively in small groups.

The First Class

Get to know your students. As students enter the class welcome them and hand them a 3- by 5-inch card (see the Figure below) for them to record information about themselves.

After class look through the cards, use them to take attendance and as the basis of later conversations. The data will help you to know if the students are in the right course. If you think the course may be too easy for some students, you might want to ask if they reviewed for the placement exam. Can they take the placement again and go to a higher course? If students have a strong background and are just taking the course for review, would they mind helping other students?

Have students chosen a reasonable load? A rule of thumb is that the number of credit hours multiplied by 3 plus the number of hours employed should resemble a full time job (40 to 45 hours per week).

For the second day of class, have a set of additional information cards for students new to the class. They can fill out the information while other students are discussing the first day's assignment.

Taking Attendance and Returning Homework

If you are required to take attendance, delete identification numbers from your class list, staple it to a piece of cardboard, and have students sign in with their initials. Before the next class, mark absent students with a yellow highlighter. Initials are distinctive enough to discourage students from signing someone else in.

Keep the attendance list and homework to be returned in a folder or set of folders—one for each group. Pass the folder around and have them sign in at the same time they retrieve their old homework from the folder.

In Class

Move around the room among the students. Teachers often talk too fast, and walking around will let you know where students are in taking

Showing your enthusiasm for mathematics and concern for your students will do more to encourage and energize them than anything else you do.

notes or working on a question. Use this time to give positive feedback, especially to those prefer taking a less active role in class discussions. When you circulate among the students during lectures or discussions you encourage their attention and participation.

This also gives you the priceless opportunity to observe how well the students are reacting to lesson. You might be amazed to see what students are doing with their class time. One reason students may initially resist working in groups in class is that they don't want to give up their freedom to use time in class as they wish.

Pay Attention to Your Timing

Don't give students something to write down and then immediately ask a thought-provoking question. It is difficult to copy information from the board and think creatively at the same time.

When you ask a question, don't look for an instant response. *Give the students time to think about the answer.* Many students mentally "check out" of a lesson because only the quick thinkers are given a chance to respond.

During questioning, respond to an answer with: "What makes you confident that your answer is correct?" This encourages reasoning and estimation by the student instead of reliance on the instructor.

Maintain a Positive Atmosphere

Showing your enthusiasm for mathematics and concern for your students will do more to encourage and energize them than anything else you do. Put yourself in the student's place and think about what you would like to hear. Better yet, go outside your world of security and learn something new to appreciate the students' efforts.

The following statements may seem stiff or scripted at first, but they really work! So, as the first statement in the list says: you can do this, try it.

- You can do this. Try it.
- Sure, the math is hard, but so are most first efforts at anything—learning to ride a bicycle, learning to sew a pattern, making

your own clay for pottery. Hard doesn't mean you can't do it.

- Be patient with yourself.
- Stuck? Be persistent.
- Let your mind work on the problem. How many times have you left a test and had an answer pop into your mind five minutes, thirty minutes, or an hour after the test?" (Delay in remembering is one reason to discourage leaving tests early.)
- Sometimes a word problem takes five or six readings before a word problem makes sense and you have found all the facts.
- It often takes more than once through material to learn it. There is nothing wrong with taking a course twice, even in your major! The author went through two-and-one-half years and a change of major between her first and second attempts at linear algebra.

Organizing Groups

The varied composition of the college population promotes the success of group work. Those re-entry students who are re-learning skills have the maturity to appreciate applications and the desire to understand concepts rather than memorize them. The re-entry student brings stability (regular attendance) to a small group and often provides patient assistance to those who have never had algebra before. The recent high school graduate adds risk-taking to the group and provides needed balance to the more conservative thinking of the re-entry student.

Organizing groups—Initially, form the groups randomly. Getting students out of their seats is a good ice breaker. Have them line up across the room by how far the classroom is from where they first remember living or by the length of time since they saw a movie in a theater. Then have them count off by the number of groups you wish to form. Another, more time-consuming but fun grouping method, is to find subsets in the class: Who knows how to play cribbage, knows how to sew, has children, has changed a tire, has had a skateboard, likes a certain kind of music, has seen a certain movie, eats breakfast.

Later on, combine abilities within groups. The AMATYC and NCTM literature contains many excellent references on group work and collaborative or cooperative learning. Change the composition of groups to accommodate different tasks or objectives.

What about students who want to go solo?—The most challenging student is the person who wishes to work in complete isolation and not participate in any group. One solution is to set up a group of those who do not wish to be in a group and instruct them to simply work by themselves, then for fun, *forbid them to talk!*

Group roles—Some instructors prefer to structure the groups by assigning members certain tasks. The leader keeps the group on task. The recorder keeps a record of conclusions by the group. The technology expert (not necessarily the person who knows the most about the technology) operates the calculator or computer or manipulative.

All members should ask questions which help guide others to learn and to figure things out themselves. The goal is *not* to give answers or "show how".

Getting Students Acquainted

Encourage students to work together before, during, and after class. Ask students to voluntarily sign up for a phone list, to be photocopied and shared with the class. (Privacy is important. Respect it.) Make a list of characteristics and have a six-minute scavenger hunt on the theme "Find someone who...". For this activity you might use such characteristics as born the same month, likes classical music, likes (the current popular music), the same kind of music you do, has not had math in five years, recently graduated from high school, is the oldest in their family, is the youngest in their family, or plays a musical instrument.

To help the students get acquainted within their groups you might have them introduce themselves to their group, give the first place they remember living (this is preferable to place of birth because some people are adopted), and state whether they have the hour before or the hour after class available for study with other students.

Encouraging group interaction—Ask students to compare strategies (rather than answers) and give hints on more thought-provoking problems. As students begin to appreciate the variety of thinking strategies others use, they will begin to appreciate that their way of thinking about a problem, while different from others, is nonetheless valid.

As basic as it may sound, remember to acknowledge and compliment groups who are at task and functioning well. You will be amazed at how effective these compliments will be in motivating less productive groups. Also, when you issue these compliments, be specific about the particular behaviors that are adding to the group's productivity: "I see that the members of your group are asking each other leading questions instead of giving answers. It appears that your questions are helping the members of your group understand the material."

When to use groups and when not to—If you are new to using peer teaching as an instructional strategy, the Section Lessons will provide you with abundant suggestions on when to lecture and when to turn the learning over to groups. It is important for you to stay within your own comfort level with any new strategy, so you may want to start out using groups gradually. When your lesson calls for summarizing material, start by having the groups do their own summaries, such as listing words that can mean subtraction in a word problem, listing steps that can be used to solve an equation, listing facts about slope, or listing ways to factor an expression. A no-talk strategy is to have each person write one item on the group list and then pass it on to the next person.

Monitoring Groups: *Don't Interrupt*

There is always a temptation to interrupt group work to clarify a point. If the instructor interrupts then the students will expect more interruptions and come to depend more on the instructor and less on themselves. Instead of interrupting, wait a few minutes to see whether the group can work through the difficulty. Suggest that the group go on to another part of their exercise or scan through the reading to look for clarification. If another group appears to have solved the difficulty, ask the second group for a hint they might share with another group on how they dealt with the issue or if it would be okay if someone from the first group came to them for help.

A five- or ten-minute overview of the expectations and directions on an assignment will prevent a thirty-minute complaint session at the next class!

For your own future approach to presenting material, make notes of useful comments or discoveries being made by the students. If all of the groups in the class are struggling with the same lesson material, take it as an indication that you need to reassess the students' readiness for the material, and perhaps do some remediation.

Calculator Teaching Aides

Set up graphing calculator teaching aides, such as posters and transparent overhead calculators on a daily basis, whether or not you plan to use it. By using these aides regularly, you will model the same behavior for students. Large calculator display posters are a great help in showing keystrokes during class discussion or in response to student inquiry.

Have students who are moderately familiar (but not expert) with the calculator volunteer to run your overhead display. This frees you to walk elsewhere in the room during calculator-based discussions. Use a laser pointer to comment on the display from a distance.

To promote success in calculator use, start by suggesting that students try a problem for which they already know the answer. Support individual investigation by arranging the seating in the class or groups to take advantage of students' existing calculator skills.

Questions on Homework

As an instructor, you need to schedule your time so you can accomplish your lesson goals and still see that a reasonable number of students get help with questions from prior assignments.

An effective strategy for reviewing homework is to approach it by objective. For example, ask the class, "Exercises 1 to 20 practiced solving equations, is there one of these that we might discuss?" Or you might say, "In the coaching yesterday I indicated that Exercises 11 to 13 are particularly important. Is there one of these exercises that we might discuss?"

As students walk into class, have them write numbers on the chalkboard of problems from the prior homework about which they have questions. Some instructors ask for a tally to seek exercises that many students want demonstrated. This avoids the domination of homework discussion by a persistent student whose individual needs are better met in a one-to-one session during your office hours.

While students do the warm-up, you decide which exercises might be incorporated into your lecture or discussion on the new topic and which will need a separate explanation. Noting the relative importance of the exercise is a good idea. If you assign priority to exercises then students will eventually also learn to recognize what is important and what is detail.

Sometimes a prior exercise makes a good lead-in to the current topic. When you are ready to move into the day's topic, review that exercise, make suggestions on how similar strategies might help on other exercises, proceed with the day's activity or material, and then go over other homework questions as you have time at the end of class. This strategy reserves a topic of high interest (how to do a given homework exercise) for the end of class when students are tired and thinking about leaving.

In all cases, acknowledge student's need to have questions answered. Encourage questions within groups or discussion with neighboring students if you are not using groups. Make an appointment for a telephone call, an e-mail, or an office visit. Encourage students to work on assignments ahead of time and to call you with questions—often a five-minute phone call can prevent an hour of frustration for the student.

Coaching on Homework

We need to coach students on what to expect when they do the reading assignments and the homework exercises. If an application setting is important, spend a few minutes talking about it (it is all right to skip some applications). A five- or ten-minute overview of the expectations and directions on an assignment will prevent a thirty-minute complaint session at the next class!

Becoming a good coach—Identify difficulties students are going to have with the homework. (If you have done the assignment yourself you will know where these stumbling block might occur.) Point out potential stumbling blocks or thought-provoking exercises. This tells the student that it is okay to struggle and be persistent on certain exercises, but it is reasonable to expect other exercises to be more straightforward. Ask students to think about the strategy for working the exercises. ●

Section Lessons

Overview

Each of the section lessons that follow contain the elements described below. The first set of elements are for the instructor's use in preparing a lesson. The second set of elements comprise the actual lesson plan.

Preparation

Objectives—These are the objectives for the section taken directly from the textbook.

Links—This list at the beginning of each section lesson shows you where to find related concepts and skills in other sections of the textbook.

Time and Emphasis—The recommended time to be spent on the section is based on a course that meets for fifty minutes, four times a week. The recommended emphasis (essential or optional) may vary according to your school's curriculum.

Vocabulary—Words that are defined for the first time in the textbook are listed in the section lesson. Occasionally, an important word from a previous section is repeated in the list.

Points to Stress—These are the instructional objectives for your lesson.

Suggested Lesson Format—Based on fifty minutes of class time, suggested lesson formats give you a minute-by-minute breakdown of the lesson. Each suggested format generally covers forty-five minutes of class time, leaving you with a five-minute "fudge factor."

Materials Needed for Class—These lists include the materials, such as sets of algebra tiles, worksheets and overhead transparencies that you will need for the lesson.

Homework—In each section you are provided with the core exercises that should be completed by every student. An expanded sample assignment includes additional exercises that are recommended for more in-depth practice for the students.

For Labs and Recitations—These recommendations are included for schools that provide additional instructional sections for students. Material for labs and recitations is intended to offer discussion and/or additional practice on difficult skills and concepts.

In Class

Warm-up—For most sections, the Warm-up from the textbook is recommended as a group activity to begin the class.

Group Activity/Lecture—This part of the lesson may also be headed "Lecture/Group Activity" depending on which style of presentation comes first in the lesson or receives the most emphasis in the lesson.

Note: The text that appears in italics offers you a suggested *script* for that part of the lesson.

Questions on Homework—Some lessons recommend reviewing the homework at the beginning of class, and others recommend covering questions on the homework at the end of class. Do whichever works best for you.

Wrap-up—The wrap-up for most section lessons includes a script to use for coaching on the homework. ●

Section 1.0 Review of Real Numbers

Preparation

Objectives
- Identify sets of numbers.
- Add, subtract, multiply, and divide integers and real numbers.
- Identify properties of real numbers.
- Use the order of operations, including square root, exponents, and absolute value.
- Match inequalities and their number line graphs.

Links
- Bases and exponents: Sections 6.0 and 6.1.
- Factoring: Sections 3.0, 3.3, 4.0, 5.3, and 5.4.
- Absolute value: Sections 2.4, 3.3, and 6.2.
- Inequalities: Sections 1.4, 3.5, and 8.6.

Time and Emphasis
50 minutes. Essential material. This lesson allows for 30 minutes of instruction and 20 minutes for "housekeeping," such as announcements, discussion of the course syllabus, and student/instructor introductions.

Vocabulary

absolute value symbol	additive inverses	associative property for multiplication
base	braces	brackets
commutative property for addition	commutative property for multiplication	compound inequality
distributive property of multiplication over addition	exponent	factor
factoring	fraction bar (horizontal)	grouping symbols
inequality	integers	irrational numbers
line graph	multiplicative inverse	natural numbers
opposites	order of operations	parentheses
power	rational numbers	real numbers
reciprocal	set	simplify
square root	symbol	undefined
whole numbers		

Points to Stress
Overview: Algebra can be studied with a four-fold approach: visual (pictures, manipulatives), numeric (tables), symbolic (algebraic notation), and verbal (writing about what we are doing, writing our conclusions). In this chapter we review these elements of the four-fold approach.

The first section has a verbal emphasis. It presents names and properties of real numbers, operations with real numbers, and an introduction to inequalities.

- Inequalities describe sets of numbers. They are used on spreadsheets to describe conditional statements and in a number of mathematical settings to describe restrictions on inputs or outputs.
- Working on algebra with a partner or in groups shows you different ways to think about the material and makes learning algebra easier and faster.

Preparation
(continued)

Suggested Lesson Format

Warm-up: 10 minutes

Lecture/Group Activity: 35 minutes

Coaching for Homework: 5 minutes

Materials Needed for Class

On the overhead or chalk board list the questions to be answered on an information/personal data card (see IRM page 9).

Review quiz *The FBI's Most Un-Wanted Errors* (IRM page 22) or a review quiz of your own.

Copies of the course syllabus.

Homework

Core exercises: 1 to 12, all (if 2 to 12 even are not done in class); 13 to 49, odd.

Sample assignment: 1 to 12, all (if 2 to 12 even are not done in class); 13 to 49, odd.

For Labs and Recitations

Create an "open syllabus" quiz that covers your course syllabus. Have students work in pairs on the quiz. Set up the pairs so one student has the syllabus and the other student has the questions and records the answers. At the halfway point, the students swap roles.

Inequality practice: Exercises 38 to 50, even, done in pairs.

In Class   **Warm-up**

(10 minutes): As the students come into the classroom, ask them to fill out an information/personal data card then work individually on the review quiz. Have them check their answers with a neighbor.

Lecture/Group Activity

(15 minutes): Introduction and course overview. Introduce yourself then discuss the course syllabus; outline your expectations; and ask the students about theirs.

(10 minutes): Review quiz. Have students discuss their answers to the review quiz in small groups (two or three students).

(10 minutes): Skills practice. Have students do Exercises 2 to 12, even, in pairs.

> **TIP** It is important that students are active in the class from the first minute they walk in on the first day. Have something for them to do immediately upon entering the room.
>
> This may be a set of review problems written on the board or overhead (see trouble spots below), or an information/personal data card.

Summarize group-work process. After the group work is finished, discuss the advantages of working in pairs or groups over working alone: *Raise your hand if you gave help or hints to someone else. Raise your hand if you received help or hints from someone else. Our backgrounds are different. Some of us will already know some material. Expect to both give and receive help throughout this course. Working together can be beneficial to everyone. The classroom is full of teachers.*

Coaching for Homework

(5 minutes): *This homework assignment helps you think about a variety of vocabulary words. Do Exercises 1 to 7, odd, without reading the section. Then skim the section to review definitions of unfamiliar vocabulary and continue with the rest of the assignment.*

NOTE Trouble Spots

Section 1.0 highlights several trouble spots. The review quiz (IRM page 000) is intended to focus the students' attention on some important details and provide a "heads-up" for students whose skills are not as good as they recall.

The trouble spots include:

- Recognizing that $\sqrt{-4}$ is not a real number, $\sqrt{-4} \neq -\sqrt{4}$ (reviewed on page 3).
- Subtracting negative numbers, (reviewed on page 4).
- Comparing $(-3)^2$ and -3^2, (reviewed on page 7).
- Using grouping symbols, (reviewed on page 10).
- Investigating why a calculator gives 11 for $(8 - \sqrt{(36)}/3 - 5$ (reviewed on page 11).
- Comparing numbers with inequalities: Use < or > between $-\frac{1}{2}$ and $-\frac{1}{4}$.

The FBI's Ten Most Un-Wanted Errors
Review Quiz

Each question in this quiz gives you the opportunity to make a common error. See how many errors you can avoid.

1. Simplify and compare: $\sqrt{-4}$ and $-\sqrt{4}$

2. Subtract: $5 - (-3)$

3. Simplify: $6 - 3(x - 7)$

4. Simplify: $(-4)^2$ and -4^2

5. Simplify: $(-2)^2$ and $-(-2)^2$

6. Are $(-x)^2$ and $-x^2$ equal?

7. Evaluate by hand and then on your calculator: $(8 - \sqrt{(36)} / (3 - 5)$

8. Evaluate by hand and then on your calculator: $(8 - \sqrt{(36)}) / (3 - 5)$

9. Compare the results in questions 7 and 8. Explain the difference in the results.

10. Simplify: $A = 5\{6 - 4[3 - 8(5 - 7) + 1] - 2\}$

Section 1.1 Input-output Tables and Expressions in Algebraic Notation

Preparation

Objectives
- Build tables and find patterns from numerical data.
- Identify variables, constants, and numerical coefficients in algebraic expressions.
- Add like terms.
- Use the simplification property of fractions to find equivalent fractions.
- Evaluate expressions and formulas.

Links
- Number patterns: Sections 2.4, 3.2, 7.0 and Appendix 2.
- Input-output tables: Section 2.1.
- Words and algebra: Section 2.1.
- Adding like terms and factoring: Section 3.0.

Time and Emphasis
50 minutes. Essential material.

Vocabulary

constant	constant term	difference
evaluate	expression	input-output relationship
like terms	numerical coefficient	product
quotient	simplify	sum
term	variable	

Points to Stress
- Review Polya's problem-solving strategies
- The common difference in a number pattern indicates the number that multiplies the input in the rule for the pattern.
- This section reviews important vocabulary and simplification the steps of adding like terms and simplifying fractions to lowest terms.
- Phrases such as *add like terms* help us distinguish terms from factors.
- Assume the difference between a and b is $a - b$, and the quotient of a and b is $a \div b$.
- Simplifying to lowest terms requires writing numerators and denominators as factors.
- Include all units in any evaluation of formulas.

Suggested Lesson Format
Warm-up: 5 minutes

Questions on Homework: 10 minutes

Lecture/Group Activity: 25 minutes

Coaching for Homework: 5 minutes

Materials Needed for Class
Overhead with patterns shown in Warm-up Exercises 1 to 5.

Homework
Core exercises: 1 to 25, odd; 31; 37 to 45, odd; 53, 55, 57, 59.

Sample assignment: 1 to 59, odd.

For Labs and Recitations

Assign Exercises 47 to 52 to be done in pairs. Pose the question: *In which exercises are parts a and b equal? Why?*

[Answer: Parts a and b are equal in Exercises 47 and 50 because when you multiply out the squared expression in part b, you get the expression in part a.]

In Class

Warm-up

(5 minutes): Assign the Warm-up to be done individually and checked with a neighbor.

Questions on Homework

(10 minutes): Have the students go over the homework in groups and select questions for class discussion.

Lecture/Group Activity

(25 minutes): Patterns and Input-Output Tables. Have the students describe their strategies for finding the next number in each Warm-up pattern. Do Examples 1 and 2 as a class and discuss how the processes they used in the Warm-up are like Polya's problem-solving steps as shown in the examples.

Define the input-output relationship. Do Example 3 as a class to show how we write the data in Examples 1 and 2 in an input-output table. Have the students make a table and find a rule for the third Warm-up pattern, as discussed in Example 4.

Vocabulary for Writing Algebraic Notation from Words. To practice vocabulary involving addition, subtraction, and equations, have the students do Examples 5 and 6 in groups. To practice vocabulary involving multiplication, division, and equations, have the students do Example 8 in groups.

Define *variable*, *constant*, *numerical coefficient*, and *expression*.

Adding Like Terms and Simplifying Expressions. Define *terms*, distinguish between terms and *factors*. To practice identifying like terms, have the students do Example 11 individually and check the Solutions in the textbook.

To practice factoring and simplifying expressions, have the students do Example 12 individually and check the Solutions in the textbook.

Evaluating Expressions and Formulas. Follow the process in the box on page 27 to evaluate a formula. Demonstrate evaluating a formula by doing Part b of Example 14.

Coaching for Homework

(5 minutes): *The homework practices each of the topics given in the Examples. Exercises 27 to 30 practice vocabulary.*

Journal Entry **Setting Up Groups**

I generally set up groups on Monday and keep these groups for the week. Since the next several sections have lots of graphing, and the use of calculators is important, grouping by the same type of calculator is helpful.

I generally assign a reader, a recorder, and a reporter for each activity so each student has a "job" during the activity. These jobs are usually assigned according to location of names in the alphabet; that way I can change the jobs each day and get everyone to do each job over the course of the week.
—LM-M

Section 1.2 Coordinate Graphs and Equations

Preparation

Objectives
- Identify horizontal and vertical axes, quadrants, the origin, and ordered pairs.
- Graph data and describe patterns in graphs.
- Build input-output tables from equations.
- Graph ordered pairs from input-output tables.
- Identify independent and dependent variables.
- Solve equations with tables and graphs.

Links
- Chapter One opens with a problem about windchill temperatures.
- Chapter Two opens with a problem about air temperature and relative humidity.
- Linear equations: Sections 2.0, 2.2, and 2.3.
- Suspension-bridge cables: Section 2.1.
- Solving equations: Sections 2.0, 3.2, 4.0, 5.6, 7.1, 8.1, and 8.5.

Time and Emphasis

50 minutes. Essential material.

Add 20 to 30 minutes if you are teaching calculator skills.

Vocabulary

axes	coordinate plane	ordered pair
origin	parabola	perpendicular
quadrants	scale	solution set
x-axis	x-coordinate	y-axis
y-coordinate		

Points to Stress
- Sets of data where one set is dependent on another can be represented by a point on the coordinate system. Graphing data in this way gives information in the form of patterns. Recognizing the patterns then allows us to predict more data points.
- Typically the data is collected, put into input-output tables, plotted and then analyzed for an equation relating the independent and dependent items. However, in mathematics, we often reverse the process in order to demonstrate what various equations look like.
- Equations that relate to data can be solved using either graphs or tables.

Suggested Lesson Format

Warm-up: 5 minutes

Questions on Homework: 10 minutes

Lecture/Group Activity: 30 minutes

Coaching for Homework: 5 minutes

Materials Needed for Class

Graphing calculator

Graph paper

Homework

Core exercises: 1 to 20, odd.

Sample assignment: Every third problem starting with Exercise 21. However, assign 40, 41 and 47 instead of 39, 42 and 48 respectively. This eliminates having the students redo earlier problems not assigned.

[For Labs and Recitations: See next page.)

> **TIP** Time Saver
> Have the instructions for activities prepared on the overhead or as handouts before class begins.

For Labs and Recitations

You can choose from one of the two lessons suggested below. Each lesson takes 20 to 30 minutes.

Motivate and reinforce coordinate graphing skills. Have the students work in pairs using guess-and-check to solve the problem: *For what values of x is $x^2 = 2^x$?* When one or two answers are found, ask: *How do we know that these are all the answers?*

We can solve equations that are impossible to solve with traditional algebraic steps. Tables and graphs provide a way! Write the tables from Example 10 on the chalkboard and have students copy and complete the tables. *What solutions can we find on the tables? What other solutions might the tables suggest?*

Next, on the graphing calculator overhead, graph $y = x^2$ and $y = 2^x$. Discuss viewing window settings (minimum, maximum, and scale) from the tables. Use -3 to 5 with a scale of 1 for the inputs, x and use -5 to 35 for the outputs y with a scale of 3.

Observe that the graphs merge together near the x-axis and it is difficult to distinguish them clearly. The graph of $y = 2^x$ rises rapidly after $x = 5$ so there are not likely to be other intersections above $x = 4$.

Adjust the window output y to -1 to 20 with a scale of 2. A third solution (point of intersection) appears between $x = -1$ and $x = 0$: *How might we have noticed this solution from the table?* [Answer: $(-1)^2$ is larger than 2^{-1} while 0^2 is smaller than 2^0.]

Next, review the vocabulary for graphing (pages 32 and 33).

To review independent and dependent variables, have the students work in pairs on Example 6: *Read and discuss Example 6, and make a sketch of axes showing the variables labeled on the axes.* [Answer: The independent variables go on the horizontal axis and the dependent variables go on the vertical axis.]

Motivation for graphing: *We can see patterns that do not appear in tables of data.* Do Examples 2 and 3 as a class and discuss the labels on the axes and the scale.

Graphing calculator skills. If graphing calculator skills are part of your curriculum, teach the techniques for plotting ordered pairs with the statistics function (page 35), and building tables and graphs (page 41).

In Class

Warm-up

(5 minutes): Assign the Warm-up to be done individually then checked with a neighbor.

Questions on Homework

(10 minutes): Have groups check their homework and select questions for class discussion.

Lecture/Group Activity

(30 minutes): Introduction. Begin with a review of the Cartesian coordinate system and how to plot points. Using either $C = 2\pi r$ or $A = \pi r^2$ as an example, construct an input-output table. Discuss the concept of independent and dependent variables in this context. Plot the points, discussing the shape of the graph. Also include a discussion of scaling and which quadrants are appropriate for use in this situation.

> **NOTE**
> Explain that graphs and tables allow us to solve equations visually. We can use this visual method as an alternative to algebraic manipulation for solving equations.
> Explaining why we are using graphs and tables helps students accept these "new" techniques.

Solving from tables or graphs. Continuing with the same equation, ask how the students might find the radius for a given circumference or area. Introduce the idea of solving equations from tables or graphs.

Students are not familiar with the concept of an equation being "dynamic." Pick several values for the circumference or area and show what this indicates graphically in terms of intersections changing both the x and y values. This will help the students better understand the connection between graphs and equations.

> **NOTE**
> Use the group activity to familiarize students with plotting points on their calculator. Assign groups so the same type of calculator is being used by each member of the group.

Group activity: This is an extension of Exercises 33 to 40, which investigate the body mass index equation.

The students will be introduced to an equation with three unknowns, fixing one of them. Besides setting up an input-output table, the students will graph the data (on calculators as well as graph paper), determining the scale and the shape of the graph.

Instruct the students to pick one member of the group as the study subject. The student gives his or her height in inches and the group generates a table of weight-and-index table, as described in the exercises. The weight values should range between 100 and 220 pounds.

Have the students enter the data into their calculators and set an appropriate window setting. This may mean handing out directions for how to do this if calculators other than the TI are being used. Ascertain ahead of time which calculators you have in your classroom.

Have the students also draw the table and graph on graph paper. (This will be the record of their work if you are using the activity for assessment purposes.) Remind the students that labels on the x- and y-axis are necessary for others to read their graphs. Give out certain values for the index and ask the students to determine what weight for their chosen height gives that index value.

If time allows and students have recognized that for a given height the data are linear, have them write the equation of the graph.

During group work. Walk around answering calculator questions and making sure the students are graphing all of the necessary information. I tend to listen or ask questions more than to answer questions during this time. The students are beginning to get some confidence in how to use their calculators. Remember to remind the students (by asking) what the independent and dependent values are for this activity.

After Group Activity. Have the groups record their tables on the board and also write the corresponding weights (and given height) for the assigned index numbers.

Coaching for Homework

(5 minutes): *Some of your answers will differ slightly from those in the answer key since they will be approximating some solutions (while using graphs or tables) rather than solving algebraically for exact solutions.*

Section 1.3 Solving Equations in One Variable and Formulas

Preparation

Objectives

- Simplify expressions containing inverse operations.
- Solve equations using inverses.
- Solve formulas using inverses.
- Check the solution to a formula.
- Apply the addition property of solving equations.
- Apply the multiplication property of solving equations.

Links

- Inverses: Sections 6.4 and 7.2.
- Formulas: Appendix 1.
- Solving formulas: Section 5.6.

Time and Emphasis

50 minutes. Essential material.

Vocabulary

additive inverses	equivalent equations	inverse order of operations
multiplicative inverse	opposites	reciprocal

Points to Stress

- The equation-solving approach here is based on Polya's problem-solving strategy of working backwards. The plan is to describe the reverse order of operations on the variable with a sequence of inverse operations.
- We check the solution to an equation by substituting the number for the variable and simplifying to an identity.
- We check the solution to a formula by substituting the expression for the variable and simplifying to an identity.

Suggested Lesson Format

Warm-up: 5 minutes
Questions on Homework: 10 minutes
Lecture/Group Activity: 30 minutes
Coaching for Homework: 5 minutes

Materials Needed for Class

Homework

Core exercises: 5; 13 to 57, odd.
Sample Assignment: 1 to 67, odd.

Avoiding the Pitfalls What *Are* You Talking About?

It is customary in algebra textbooks to label the answer to an example as the "solution," which is not correct in the strictest sense.

In algebra, we restrict the meaning of the word *solve* to "describe the steps we use to isolate the variable in an equation." We use the word *simplify* to mean we are doing operations with expressions. However, one side of an equation, that is, an expression, can be simplified in the process of solving an equation. We use *evaluate* to describe placing numbers or expressions into equations, formulas, expressions (and, later, functions).

No wonder students get confused!

Remind students to use the quick reference (just inside the front cover of the textbook) to help them understand the instructions to "solve," "simplify," or "evaluate."

For Labs and Recitations

Practice solving equations and formulas:

Solve $S = a + b(c - d)$ for each of a, b, c, and d
Repeat for $S = a - b(c + d)$.

Note: It is helpful to change $c - d$ to $c + (-d)$ and $a - b$ to $a - b$ when setting up the plan.

In Class   **Warm-up**

(5 minutes): Have the students do the following Warm-up individually: List the choices you have for doing the first step in solving the formula in Part a, and the equation in Part b.

   a. Solve the formula $A = \frac{1}{2}h(a + b)$ for a.

   b. Solve the equation $9 - 4(x - 6) = 21$ for x (from Example 6).

[Answers: a. Multiply both sides by 2; or multiply both sides by $\frac{2}{h}$; or distribute $\frac{2}{h}$ over $a + b$. b. Subtract 9 from each side; or change $9 - 4$ to $9 + (-4)$ and distribute $[(-4)$ over $x - 6]$.

Questions on Homework

(10 minutes): Discuss the homework exercises selected by the students.

Lecture/Group Activity

(30 minutes): Give the students five minutes to discuss the Warm-up in groups of three. Have each group to list three different first steps for the formula and the equation. Discuss the three first steps with the whole class. (More than three may be possible, and all reasonable choices should be listed.) Not very many students can initially solve the formula.

The students' first steps will likely mention the properties of equations or properties of real numbers. Write the properties and remind students how the inverses (opposites and reciprocals) transform the equations. It may be useful to do Examples 1 and 2 as a class.

Most importantly, remind students that the properties of equations justify the steps and show that the results are equal. But they don't answer the most important questions in solving formulas and equations: *Where do we start?* and *In what order do we do the steps?*

> *Journal Entry* **When All Else Fails**
> If students can't solve the formula (or don't even know where to begin), I insist that they switch to the inverse order of operations method: List the operations as they are applied to the variable in the original equation or formula, then reverse the order and list the inverse operation.   —AK

Reversing the order of inverse operations. For the formula in the Warm-up, the variable b is <u>added</u> to a, the sum is <u>multiplied</u> by h, and the product is <u>divided</u> by 2. We use the reverse order of inverse operations to <u>multiply</u> by 2 (on both sides), <u>divide</u> by h (on both sides) and then <u>subtract</u> b (on both sides).

> **Avoiding the Pitfalls**
> Keep in mind that your students are learning a mathematical process at the same time they are learning the vocabulary that describes what they are doing.
> Some students may need some "think time" to mentally process the concepts of *opposites, inverses,* and *inverse order of operations* during the lesson.

Inverse order of operations. Remind the students that the properties of equations apply to *addition* and *multiplication*. Therefore, to solve the equation $9 - 4(x - 6) = 21$, we *change subtraction to addition* of the opposite: $9 + (-4)(x + (-6)) = 21$.

   In other words, the operations on x are: add -6, multiply by -4, then add 9. The inverse order of operations is to subtract 9, divide by -4, and add 6 (or subtract -6).

Have students practice solving equations using the inverse order of operations by solving $P = 2\ell + 2w$ for w (from Example 9) and $\frac{5}{9}(x - 32) = 100$ (from Example 7).

Remind them to check their work (see Examples 13 and 14 for checking formulas).

Coaching for Homework

(5 minutes): *The exercises focus on equations with variables on one side only. To facilitate use of the inverse order of operations, equations with variables on both sides must first be changed (with the addition property) to equations with variables on one side.*

In the exercises that call for solving equations or formulas, be sure to include the following steps: Copy the equation or formula. Show the inverse-operation steps you use solving the equation and formula. State your conclusion as: x = a number, or, for a formula, variable *= an expression. Show the check.*

Section 1.4 Solving Inequalities in One and Two Variables

Preparation

Objectives

- Solve inequalities in one variable with graphs and with algebraic notation.
- Find the number-line solution to one-variable inequalities.
- Write inequalities in two variables to describe quadrants and axes.
- Graph inequalities in two variables on coordinate axes.

Links

- Inequalities: 1.0, 3.5, and 8.6.

Time and Emphasis

50 minutes. Essential material.

Vocabulary

boundary line   equivalent inequalities

Points to Stress

- We can solve inequalities by graphing.
- A test point is a graphical guess-and-check and is essential in solving inequalities from a graph.
- The solution set for a one-variable inequality is shown on a graph and summarized on the number line (see Figures 22 and 23 on pages 59 and 60).
- The solution set for a two-variable inequality is summarized with shading on a coordinate graph.
- Inequalities in one variable may be solved with algebraic notation.
- Avoiding multiplication or division of both sides of an inequality by a negative reduces the likelihood of an error.

Suggested Lesson Format

Warm-up: 5 minutes

Questions on Homework: 15 minutes

Lecture/Group Activity: 25 minutes

Coaching for Homework: 5 minutes

Materials Needed for Class

Graphing Calculator Overhead Projection Unit

Homework

Core exercises: 15 to 23, odd; 29, 31; 35 to 51, odd.

Sample assignment: 1 to 55, odd.

Note: Include Exercise 57 if compound inequalities are part of your curriculum.

For Labs and Recitations

For solving compound inequalities, do the project in Exercise 57.

Review Exercises 1 to 12 (page 70).

In Class **Warm-up**

(5 minutes): Assign the Warm-up to be done individually.

Questions on Homework

(15 minutes): Have the students correct the homework in groups and select two exercises to be discussed by the class.

Lecture/Group Activity

(25 minutes): Solving one-variable inequalities by graphing. Have the students work in pairs on Example 1.

Discuss *Solving an Inequality: Method 1* (Textbook page 58) and *Solving an Inequality: Method 2* (page 59): The difference is that Method 1 uses a test point to mark the solution's direction on the number line and Method 2 uses the relative position of the graphs in the on the coordinate plane to find the solution's direction on the number line.

Multiplication properties of inequalities. To motivate the multiplication properties of inequalities, have the students work in pairs on the exploration in Example 7 and write out their own rules based on the example. Discuss their results as a class.

Solving inequalities in two variables. Extend solving inequalities by graph to include inequalities in two variables: *To solve inequalities in two variables, we graph the inequality, then use a test point to find and shade the half-plane that summarizes the solution.*

Use Example 11 and/or Exercise 52 as problem settings for pairs of students to explore solving inequalities in two variables by graph.

Coaching for Homework

(5 minutes): *The solutions to the one-variable inequalities in Exercises 1 to 14 are described in terms of Method 2. Exercises 15 to 24 may be solved with either Method 1 or Method 2.*

The inequalities in Exercises 35 to 38 are to be interpreted as two-variable inequalities.

Section 2.0 Writing and Solving Linear Equations

Preparation

Objectives
- Apply Polya's problem-solving steps.
- Build linear equations with guess and check.
- Write linear equations from word statements containing conditions.
- Graph linear equations containing conditions.
- Solve linear equations from graphs.

Links
- Polya's problem-solving steps: Section 1.1.
- Guess and check: Sections 2.3, 6.1, and 8.0.
- Conditional equations (domain and range in functions): Section 2.1.

Time and Emphasis

50 minutes. Essential material.

Vocabulary

| condition | dot graph | linear equation in one variable |

step graph

Points to Stress

- The problem-solving steps used to identify rules for patterns, Section 1.1, also apply to building equations from word-problem settings. In this section we emphasize the guess-and-check strategy, which can also be done systematically on a graphing calculator.

- Real world settings often have conditions on the inputs. These conditions are included in the resulting equations and are the basis for dot graphs and step graphs.

> **NOTE** Step graphs are usually described with the greatest integer function, but this function is not in the intermediate algebra curriculum. In my experience, students are quite comfortable with the concept that step graphs result from rounding the inputs. Stressing the graphical result avoids burdening them with unfamiliar vocabulary. —AK

- Dot graphs result from the condition that inputs are limited to integers.
- Step graphs result from the condition that inputs containing fractions or decimals are rounded up to the next highest integer.

Suggested Lesson Format

Warm-up: 5 minutes

Questions on Homework: 10 minutes

Lecture/Group Activity: 25 minutes

Coaching for Homework: 10 minutes

Materials Needed for Class

Homework

Core exercises: 1 to 25, odd.

Sample assignment: 1 to 25, odd.

For Labs and Recitations

Start this lesson with a game of Twenty Questions. For example, *On this piece of paper, I have written a number between 1 and 1,000,000. What is my number? You have twenty guesses, and I can answer only yes or no.* Suppose your number is 498,366. Students will observe that they can save on questions by asking for ranges of numbers, instead of making individual number guesses. Halving the interval containing the number should always find the number in twenty guesses.

Next, explore guess-and-check on the graphing calculator. The calculator replay key can be used to do guess-and-check in a similar manner to the tables. For Example 1, enter 12 times the guess + 1.5, times 10 times the guess, and look for 2160 as the output. Replay to enter a new guess. For Example 2, enter 28 times the guess, add 22 and 85, then look for 205 as an output.

In Class

Warm-up

(5 minutes): Assign the Warm-up to be done and checked in groups.

Questions on Homework

(10 minutes): Have the students go over the homework in groups and select questions for class discussion.

Lecture/Group Activity

(25 minutes): Building linear equations through guess-and-check. Do Example 1 and model the guess-and-check strategy for the class. Ask a student at random for his or her birth date to use to start the process of filling out Table 2 on page 76. Build an equation, as modeled in Table 3. Have students work in pairs to do Exercise 6 by guess-and-check.

Writing linear equations with conditions. Define *condition*, (see textbook page 78). Do Example 3 as a class to illustrate writing conditions for word settings. Write equations from the conditional settings in Examples 4 and 5.

Graphs of linear equations with conditions. Have the students work in pairs to graph the data from Example 4 and part a of Example 5. Discuss results and dot graphs (where the inputs are positive integers).

In pairs, graph the data from parts b and c of Example 5. Discuss step graphs (where the inputs are rounded to integers).

Coaching for Homework

(10 minutes): *When you write the equations in Exercises 7 to 16, define the variables by stating their meaning and units. This avoids writing units (and dollar signs) within the equations.*

> **TIP** Many students fear making a mistake, even when guessing. Encourage these students to guess their birthday as a means of getting started. Since the birth date is an arbitrary number, there is no stigma attached to the number being way off from a reasonable guess.
>
> A birth date is not logical, so the purpose of the birthday as first guess is not to get the right answer but to help read and understand the problem setting. The birthday guess may, however, give useful information for making the next guess.

Section 2.1 Functions

Preparation
Day One of Two

Objectives (Day One)
- Identify a function.
- Describe a relationship with functions.
- Graph functions on coordinate axes.
- Apply the vertical-line test.

Links (Day One)
- Functions: Sections 2.4, 3.1, 3.2, 6.4, 7.0, 7.1, and 7.2.
- Inverse variation (mirror activity): Section 5.2.

Time and Emphasis
Two 50-minute sessions. Essential material.

Vocabulary

range	relevant domain	relevant range
vertical-line test		

Points to Stress
- Functions may be described with a graph, a written rule, a listing of ordered pairs, or an equation.
- A relationship is identified as a function from its ordered pairs or table (exactly one output for each input) or its graph (passing the vertical-line test).
- Functions may be visualized as putting numbers or objects through a function machine or as mapping one set of numbers or objects onto another set.

Suggested Lesson Format (Day One)
Warm-up: 15 minutes
Lecture/Group Activity: 20 minutes
Questions on Homework: 10 minutes
Coaching for Homework: 5 minutes

Materials Needed for Class
Mirrors
Protractors
Copies of *Mirror, Mirror* (IRM page 36)

Homework
Core exercises: 1 to 23, odd.

Sample assignment: 1 to 23, all; 63 and 64 with algebraic notation only.

Select 5 ordered pairs on the graphs in Exercises 13 to 18. Make a mapping with the ordered pairs and explain how the mapping shows whether the graphs illustrate functions.

Draw a mapping for each of Exercises 19 to 24.

For Labs and Recitations

Sharp Pencils activity (IRM page 40). This project for exploring functions is based on activities created by Joel Teller of the College Preparatory School, Oakland, California and presented at the California Mathematics Council Conference (December 1991).

Materials needed: Five identical pencils with erasers, a scale calibrated in grams, a metric ruler, and graph paper.

In Class

(Day One)

Warm-up

(15 minutes): Have the students work in groups of three to do the exploration in *Mirror, Mirror* activity. Remind students of the assumption that we count the original object as one of the objects.

Lecture/Group Activity

(20 minutes): Defining functions. Include discussion questions about the mirror table with an introduction of the function concept: *We say that the number of objects is a function of the angle between the mirrors.*

> **NOTE** The purpose of the mirror activity at this time is to develop the function concept, not to find a formula for the relationship between the angles and the number of objects. Permit students to explore the relationship on their own. We will return to the mirrors for inverse variation in Section 5.2. The rule is the number of objects is 360 divided by the number of degrees. We may also say that the product of the number of objects and the number of degrees is constant, 360.

Identifying functions from ordered pairs (tables) or from a graph. Do Examples 2 and 3 with the class and introduce the vertical-line test. Have students work in pairs on Example 4.

Visualizing functions. Do Example 5 with the class: *We can visualize functions with a function machine.* Do Example 6 with the class: *We can also visualize functions with a mapping.*

Function notation. Explain to the class that we have special notation for functions, $f(x)$. Our set of inputs to a function is associated with the horizontal axis, or x-axis. Our set of outputs to a function is associated with the vertical axis, or y-axis. Thus we often say that a function is $y = f(x)$. Have students read Example 7 in pairs.

Questions on Homework

(10 minutes): Have the students go over the homework in groups and select questions for class discussion.

Coaching for Homework

(5 minutes): *The homework assignment is based on the class discussion and Examples 1 to 7.*

Mirror, Mirror

<u>Materials needed</u>: A protractor, two mirrors, and a pencil or pen.

<u>Instructions</u>: Place a protractor flat on your desk. Place two mirrors on the protractor in a V shape with one mirror along the 0-degree line of the protractor, the other mirror on the 60-degree mark, and the center of the V at the center of the protractor (see the figure below). Finally, place an object such as a pencil between the two mirrors.

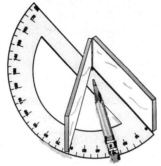

<u>Activity</u>:

1. Count the number of pencils seen in the mirror plus the pencil itself. Record this number on the table below. Move the second mirror to the angles shown on the table and record the number of pencils you see (always count the actual pencil as one of the objects seen). For the last two entries, move the mirror to positions of your own choosing.

Angle Between the Mirrors	Number of Objects
120°	
90°	
60°	6
45°	
30°	

2. As you change the angle between the mirrors, what happens to the number of objects seen?

3. As you make the angle between the mirrors smaller, what happens to the number of objects seen?

4. What is the largest possible angle between the mirrors for this activity?

5. Is there a smallest angle between the mirrors?

Sharp Pencils

<u>Materials needed</u>: Five identical new pencils with erasers, a scale calibrated in grams, a metric ruler, and graph paper.

<u>Instructions</u>: Sharpen the pencils to different lengths.

<u>Activity</u>:

1. After you have sharpened the pencils, make the following *predictions*:

    a. If you graph the mass of each pencil in grams as a function of its length in centimeters, what shape will the graph have?

    b. What unit describes the steepness, or slope, of the graph?

    c. What is the meaning of the *y*-intercept?

2. Set up an input-output table with the mass of a pencil as a function of its length.

3. Draw a graph by plotting mass as a function of length.

    a. Explain the shape of the graph.

    b. If you were to repeat the experiment with a different brand of pencil, how might the resulting graph change? How might the resulting graph be the same?

    c. What would be the effect on the graph of cutting the erasers off the pencils?

    d. What other questions might be asked about this activity?

    e. What other variations on this activity could you try?

Preparation
(Day Two of Two)

Objectives (Day Two)
- Evaluate functions written in function notation.
- Find the domain and range of a function.

Links (Day Two)
- Linear function: Section 2.2.
- Squaring binomials: Section 3.4.
- Function notation and intercepts: Section 4.1.
- Evaluation: Section 4.5.

Time and Emphasis
Two 50-minute sessions. Essential material.

Vocabulary

range   relevant domain   relevant range
vertical-line test

Points to Stress
- Evaluate functions by substituting the input for x into the function described by $f(x)$.
- Describe relationships between outputs to functions with function notation as in $f(x) = x^2, f(-2) = f(2)$
- The domain and range describe the sets of inputs and outputs to a function.
- The domain and range of a mathematical function may be limited in application settings to a relevant domain and relevant range.

Suggested Lesson Format
Warm-up: 5 minutes
Questions on Homework: 10 to 15 minutes
Lecture/Group Activity: 25 minutes
Coaching for Homework: 5 minutes

Materials Needed for Class
None

Homework
Core exercises: 25 to 47, odd.
Sample assignment: 25 to 36, all; 37 to 67, odd.

For Labs and Recitations
Mass and Cardboard Circle activity (IRM page 40). This project for exploring functions is based on activities created by Joel Teller of the College Preparatory School, Oakland, California and presented at the California Mathematics Council Conference (December 1991).

Materials needed: A piece of cardboard, a compass, a metric ruler, a scale calibrated in grams, scissors, and graph paper.

In Class **Warm-up**
(Day Two) (5 minutes): Assign the Warm-up to be done individually.
Questions on Homework
(10 to 15 minutes): Have the students go over the homework in groups and select questions for class discussion.
Lecture/Group Activity
(25 minutes): Evaluating functions and function notation. *The exercises in the Warm-up return to the suspension bridge and transcripts equations from Section 1.2.* Explain that when the students completed the tables for Exercises 1 and 3 in the Warm-up, they evaluated functions. If an equation is a function, we say $y = f(x)$. For Warm-up Exercise 1, $f(x) = 3 + 2(x - 1)$. The outputs were $f(1) = 3$, $f(2) = 5$, $f(3) = 7$, $f(4) = 9$, and $f(5) = 11$.

For Exercise 2, $f(x) = \dfrac{4}{125}x^2$, $f(-20) = 12.8$, $f(-10) = 3.2$, $f(0) = 0$, $f(10) = 3.2$, $f(20) = 12.8$. The suspension-bridge function is evaluated for additional inputs in Example 9. Have the students do Example 8 in pairs and then make a mapping for the alarm clock function.

Inputs to functions can be variables as well as numbers or words. Place the inputs to the function in Example 10 in a table and then have the students complete the table and do Example 10. This reinforces the concept that $y = f(a)$ when the input is a, $x = a$.

> **NOTE** Geometric transformations (reflection, rotation, translation, dilation, similarity) are functions that have sets of points in the plane (or space) as their domains. Their ranges are also sets of points.

> **Avoiding the Pitfalls**
> Domain and range are difficult concepts. Approach them as describing sets of inputs and sets of outputs. For most of the course, use both the set descriptions and the domain and range so that students continually make the association.

Domain and range. The domain, or set of inputs, for the mirror table is the angle measures, 0 to 180. The range, or set of outputs, is the number of objects, $y \geq 1$.

Remind students about restrictions they have already seen, such as the definition of rational numbers ($\dfrac{a}{b}$, where a and b are integers, and $b \neq 0$) because of the restriction on division by zero.

We use inequalities to describe the domains and ranges. We use $\Re$ to name the set of all real numbers. Have students complete the following table individually and check in pairs.

Function	Domain (set of inputs)	Range (set of outputs)
$y = \sqrt{x}$		
$y = x^2$		
$y = |x|$		

[Answers: Domains $x \geq 0$, $\Re$, $\Re$, ranges all $y \geq 0$.]

Coaching for Homework
(5 minutes): *Exercises 35 and 36 include squaring expressions. We will review and do more with $(a + b)^2 = a^2 + 2ab + b^2$ in Section 3.0 and 3.4. Exercises 63 to 68 review solving equations with tables.*

Mass and Cardboard Circle

<u>Materials needed</u>: A piece of cardboard, a compass, a metric ruler, a scale calibrated in grams, scissors, and graph paper.

<u>Instructions</u>: On the cardboard, draw five concentric circles (circles with the same center) of random radii. Then trim the cardboard to the outermost circle.

<u>Activity</u>:

1. After you have trimmed the cardboard around the outermost circle, make the following *predictions*:

    a. If you graph the mass of each circle in grams as a function of its radius in centimeters, what shape will the graph have?

    b. What unit describes the steepness, or slope, of the graph?

    c. What is the meaning of the *y*-intercept?

2. Set up an input-output table with mass of a circle as a function of its radius. Measure and record the radius of the outermost circle. Measure and record the mass of the outermost circle. Then cut off the outer ring of the cardboard. Continue measuring and recording the radius and mass of each circle down to the smallest one.

3. Draw a graph by plotting the mass as a function of radius.

    a. Is the shape of the graph in this project the same as the graph in the *Sharp Pencils* project?

    b. What would be the effect on the graph of placing a tack in the center of each circle?

    c. What would be the effect on the graph of cutting a hole in the center of the concentric circles?

    d. What other questions might be asked about this activity?

    e. What other variations on this activity could you try?

Section 2.2 Linear Functions

Preparation   **Objectives**
- Find *x*- and *y*-intercepts of the graph of a linear function.
- Identify a linear function from a linear equation.
- Identify increasing and decreasing linear functions.
- Find the slope of a linear function from data points, a table, and a graph.
- Find the meaning of slope in an application setting.
- Find the slope of vertical and horizontal lines.
- Identify parallel and perpendicular lines.

Links
- Functions: Section 2.1.
- Linear functions: Section 2.3.
- Functions and intercepts: Section 4.1.

Time and Emphasis
50 minutes. Essential material. You may want to spend more time on this section if the students' $y = mx + b$ skills are weak.

Vocabulary

conditional function	increasing function	linear function
nonvertical	slope	subscripts
x-intercept	*y*-intercept	

Points to Stress
- How to determine whether a function is linear.
- How to find the *x*- and *y*-intercepts (always denote these as ordered pairs).
- How to find slope.
- What slope means.
- Identify negative and positive slopes, and parallel and perpendicular slopes.

Suggested Lesson Format
Warm-up: 10 minutes
Lecture/Group Activity: 35 minutes
Coaching for Homework: 5 minutes

Materials Needed for Class
Refer to your calculator manual for details on programming instructions.
Overhead transparency of *What Makes a Function Linear?*(IRM page 43).

Homework
Core exercises: 1 to 25, odd.
Sample assignment: 1 to 47, odd.

For Labs and Recitations
Have the students write, enter, and practice a program for finding the slope given two ordered pairs. Use the program to repeat Examples 9, 10, 11, and 12. For example, a program for slope through ordered pairs (A, B) and (C, D) might be:

```
PROGRAM: SLOPE
:[Prompt] A,B,C,D
:(D-B)/(C-A)[STO]M
:[Disp]M
```

In Class

Warm-up

(10 minutes): Assign the Warm-up to be done individually and checked in groups. Ask the students if they remember *what* this process asks them to find. Many students may remember that this is the way to determine the slope of a line. Extend the warm-up by asking the students to work in groups to plot the points. Use their results to discuss *zero*, *undefined*, *positive* and *negative slopes*. In addition, for the values which are positive, talk about which line segment is "steeper."

Lecture/Group Activity

(35 minutes): Slope and linear functions. Review the form of a line, $y = mx + b$. Remind the students that, with the exception of an undefined slope, this is a function (good time for a function review!), which can be written as $f(x) = mx + b$.

To get at the idea of linearity, complete the tables on the transparency *What Makes a Function Linear*. Emphasize that the constant ratio $\dfrac{\Delta x}{\Delta y}$ makes a linear function linear! This table also introduces the *difference* concept with the delta x, Δx, and delta y, Δy. Have the students graph both functions to really "see" what the difference between linear and not linear looks like.

Intercepts. Refer to Example 9 to talk about the significance of intercepts. This is a good practical example of what both the x- and y-intercepts mean. Talk about using $y = 0$ and $x = 0$ to find each of these intercepts, given an equation.

Parallel and perpendicular lines. Remind the students how to identify parallel and perpendicular lines by their slopes. For most students this is a review, so rather than giving examples, this is included in the group activity.

Group activity. Assign Exercise 44 to be done in groups. Add the following instructions to the exercise:

> *Journal Entry* I have the students work in small groups on Exercise 44 so they can split up the number of slopes they need to calculate.

   a. Do not assume the figures are square, even though they appear to be.
   b. Plot the points on graph paper and connect the points.
   c. Find the slope of each line segment.
   d. Which are the same slope? What does this mean about the segments?
   e. Which have slope products that are −1? What does this mean about the segments?

If time allows, have the students work on Exercises 36 and 40.

Summary. Emphasize the physical and applied meanings of both the slope and the intercepts. It is also good to remind the students what a linear function is (again!).

Coaching for Homework

(5 minutes): A warning here about Exercises 15 to 22: , the students have a difficult time with the language "for $x < 0$" when describing what the y-values are doing. It may be a good idea to do Exercise 22 for the class if time allows.

What Makes a Function Linear?

Δx	x	$f(x)$	Δy	$\dfrac{\Delta x}{\Delta y}$
	−1	−1		
	0	2		
	2	8		
	3	11		
	4.5	15.5		

Δx	x	$g(x)$	Δy	$\dfrac{\Delta x}{\Delta y}$
	−1	11		
	0	6		
	2	2		
	3	3		
	4.5	8.25		

Section 2.3 Modeling with a Linear Function

Preparation

Objectives
- Find a linear equation using the slope-intercept equation.
- Find a linear equation using the point-slope equation.
- Find a linear equation using the line of best fit.
- Find a linear equation using calculator regression.

Links
- Slope and intercepts: Section 2.2.
- Calculator regression: Sections 4.1 and 7.0.

Time and Emphasis
50 minutes. Essential material.

Vocabulary

coefficient of correlation   line of best fit   linear regression
modeling with a linear function   point-slope equation
slope-intercept equation

Points to Stress
- If we define variables with units then there is no need to put units or dollar signs in our equations.
- The slope-intercept equation is only one of four methods of finding the equation of a line through a set of data. It is closely related to the point-slope method.
- The *line of best fit* is a guess-and-check method of finding an equation using either slope-intercept or point-slope method. Calculator regression is a statistical method resulting in an equation in slope-intercept form.

Suggested Lesson Format
Warm-up: 5 minutes
Questions on Homework: 10 minutes
Lecture/Group Activity: 30 minutes
Coaching for Homework: 5 minutes

Materials Needed for Class
None

Homework
Core exercises: 1 to 21, odd; 25 to 29, odd; 37 to 45 odd.
Sample assignment: 1 to 51, odd.

Optional Activities
Fit equations to data about diamonds from advertising brochures enclosed in newspapers from local jewelry stores. You may have luck calling these stores and finding current prices for diamonds such as those described in Exercise 51. Fit equations by various methods to the data.

For Labs and Recitations
Hours of Sleep (IRM page 46)
Discuss which of the four methods of finding a linear equation
are appropriate by doing the project in Exercise 53.

In Class   **Warm-up**

(5 minutes): Assign the Warm-up to be done individually.

Questions on Homework

(10 minutes): Have the students go over the homework in groups and select questions for class discussion.

Lecture/Group Activity

(30 minutes): Slope-intercept linear equation. Review slope and *y*-intercept and introduce the slope-intercept linear equation with Example 1 and Examples 4 and 5. Have them solve for *y*-intercept (Think About It 1), to reinforce solving formulas as a method to save repeatedly substituting and solving the resulting equations. Have the students do Examples 2 and 3.

> **NOTE**
> Because we have a formula for slope, students find it more natural to have a formula for *y*-intercept instead of substituting and solving in the slope-intercept equation.

Point-slope equation. The point-slope equation, Example 7, permits finding the equation before finding the *y*-intercept from two ordered pairs. Because calculator regression quickly gives the slope-intercept equation of a line from two ordered pairs, some instructors reduce the emphasis on the point-slope equation. However, if it is an essential part of your curriculum, the point-slope form is useful in finding equations for lines parallel or perpendicular to other lines, as shown in Example 8.

Line of best fit. Both line of best fit and calculator regression are methods to fit an equation to a set of data containing more than two ordered pairs. The watts and lumen data, Example 9, from light bulbs give surprisingly linear results. Because the lumen data varies with the materials used in manufacturing light bulbs, the data on packages you find in the store may vary from the data in the text.

Linear regression. Be sure to include Figure 30 in any discussion of the coefficient of correlation that appears on the calculator when doing regression. Students generally understand when $r = -1$ or $r = +1$ are related to negatively and positively sloped lines. Example 10 returns to the light bulb data.

Coaching for Homework

(5 minutes): *In economics and accounting, the slope-intercept linear equations may be written, $C = Vx + F$, as used in Exercises 23, 24, 31, and 32.*

In Exercises 48 to 51, use either line of best fit or calculator regression.

> **TIP** Avoid 1 or –1 Slope
> When you make up examples or test items, be sure to avoid using slopes of 1 or –1, as these values would prevent students from finding correct slope from change in *x* over change in *y*.

Hours of Sleep

<u>Materials needed</u>: Graph paper.

<u>Activity</u>: Suppose you go to bed at 7 P.M. or later and your alarm is set for 6 A.M.

    a. Make a graph with time to bed as the input and hours of sleep as the output.

    b. Use algebraic notation to describe the hours of sleep as a function of the time to bed.

    c. Use algebraic notation to describe the hours of sleep as a function of the number of hours after 6 P.M. that you go to bed.

<u>Consider this</u>: Look at the graph below. Because the x-axis is not labeled 0 to 12, the x inputs behave differently than they do in ordinary graphs.

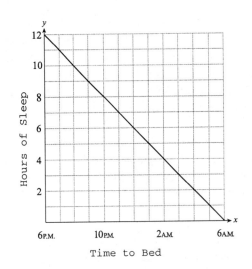

The answer to Part b is a conditional statement:

        If x is between 6 P.M. and 1 A.M., $y = 6 - (x - 12)$ hours of sleep.

        If x is between 1 A.M. and 6 A.M., $y = 6 - x$.

The answer to Part c is $y = 12 - x$. The moral of the story is that how we label the x-axis can make a considerable difference in the equations!

Section 2.4 Special Functions

Preparation

Objectives
- Find a linear equation from a sequence.
- Find a specified term of a sequence based on a linear function.
- Identify and graph constant and identity functions.
- Identify and graph absolute value functions.
- Find the domain and range of special functions.

Links
Sequences: Sections 1.1, 3.2, 4.1, 7.0, and Appendix 2.
Absolute value: Sections 1.0, 3.3, and 6.2.

Time and Emphasis
50 minutes. Essential material.

Vocabulary

absolute value function	arithmetic sequence	common difference
identify function	rule for the nth term of a sequence	

> **NOTE** In most textbooks, no connection is made between sequences and linear equations. The connection is made here because sequences provide a numerical method for recognizing and distinguishing different types of functions (linear functions, quadratic functions, and exponential functions).
>
> Sequences also permit us to motivate domain because the domain of a sequence is the positive integers while the domain of a linear function is all real numbers.

Points to Stress
- Number patterns or sequences help us distinguish different types of functions. We have seen how finding the change in y and change in x in a table finds the slope of a linear function. From here on we will use changes or differences to identify types of functions.
- Sequences with constant differences may be described with either an nth term expression or a linear equation. The term a_n of a sequence of numbers may be paired with a natural number to form an ordered pair, (n, a_n).
- A constant function has a horizontal graph and an equation $y = c$, where c is a real number.
- The graph of the identity function is the line $y = x$.
- The absolute value function describes the distance a number is from zero on the number line.

Suggested Lesson Format
Warm-up: 5 minutes
Questions on Homework: 10 minutes
Lecture/Group Activity: 30 minutes
Coaching for Homework: 5 minutes

Materials Needed for Class
None

Homework
Core exercises: 5 to 13, odd; 17 to 37, odd.
Sample assignment: 1 to 43, odd.

For Labs and Recitations
Absolute Value and Inequalities activity (IRM page 49).

In Class

Warm-up

(5 minutes): Assign the Warm-up to be done individually then checked with a neighbor.

Questions on Homework

(10 minutes): Have the students check the homework in groups and select questions for class discussion.

Lecture/Group Activity

(30 minutes): Sequences. Discuss the answers to the Warm-up, then discuss *differences*, based on Example 1. Explain how to match the number in the sequence with its position, a natural number, in an ordered pair, (n, a_n), based on Example 2. Have the students work in groups to graph the ordered pairs (as done in Example 3) and predict the equations in the form $y = mx + b$, if possible, for the sequences in Warm-up Exercises 1 to 4.

Do Example 4 with the class to show finding the equation or rule for a sequence in another way and lead to the nth term of a sequence formula, $a_n = a_1 + (n -- 1)d$. Apply the nth term to finding a specific term, Example 7.

If time, have students apply this rule to other Warm-up sequences with common differences and compare their results with their equations $y = mx + b$.

Other Functions: constant, identity, and absolute value. Introduce constant and identity functions. Do Example 10 in groups.

Introduce absolute value function and have student groups use graphing calculators to do Example 12.

Coaching for Homework

(5 minutes): *Exercises 1 to 16 involve sequences.*

Exercises 17 to 28 involve identity and constant functions.

Exercises 29 to 44 focus on absolute value functions.

Optional Activities

Intervals: We introduce intervals in Section 4.5, however, you may mention them here in the context of domain and range.

Probability and Probability Functions:

The projects in Exercises 45 and 46 introduce probability functions related to rolling dice. A third probability function results from flipping a coin. The outcome for a coin flip is "heads or tails," which is the input to the probability function. The probability of each outcome is $\frac{1}{2}$, so this is the output corresponding to each input in the probability function. More formally, the domain is {heads, tails} and the range is $\{\frac{1}{2}\}$.

Note the subtle distinction between *outcome* and *output*. A fourth probability function is the absolute value of difference between the top faces on a pair of rolled dice, see *Dice Differences*, (IRM page 50).

Absolute Value and Inequalities

<u>Materials needed</u>: Graph paper.

<u>Activity</u>:

From the statements in a through d, make a table with integer inputs between –5 and 5.

    a.   If $x \leq 3$, output is $3 - x$. If $x > 3$, output is $x - 3$.

    b.   If $x < -3$, output is $-x - 3$. If $x \geq -3$, output is $x + 3$.

    c.   If $x < -2$, output is $x + 2$. If $x \geq -2$, output is $-x - 2$.

    d.   If $x \leq \frac{1}{2}$, output is $2x - 1$. If $x > \frac{1}{2}$, output is $1 - 2x$.

Use the graphing calculator to compare the choices in Parts e through h.

    e.   Which of these absolute value equations is another name for the graph in Part a?

$$y = |x + 3| \qquad\qquad y = -|x - 3| \qquad\qquad y = |x - 3|$$

    f.   Which of these absolute value equations is another name for the graph in Part b?

$$y = |x + 3| \qquad\qquad y = -|x - 3| \qquad\qquad y = |3 - x|$$

    g.   Which of these absolute value equations is another name for the graph in Part c?

$$y = -|x + 2| \qquad\qquad y = |x - 2| \qquad\qquad y = |x + 2|$$

    h.   Which of these absolute value equations is another name for the graph in Part d?

$$y = -|2x - 1| \qquad\qquad y = |2x - 1| \qquad\qquad y = |1 + 2x|$$

Dice Differences

Materials needed: Graph paper

Activity: Suppose you have two dice, each with sides numbered from 1 to 6.

    a. Complete the first table with the absolute value of the difference for each possible roll of the dice?

	1	2	3	4	5	6
0						
1	0					
2						
3						
4						
5						
6						

    b. Use the table of differences to complete the Number of Outcomes column in the second table.

Absolute Value of Difference, n	Number of Outcomes	Probability Function, $P(n)$
0	6	$\frac{6}{36} = \frac{1}{6}$
1		
2		
3		
4		
5		

    c. From the Number of Outcomes column, find the total possible outcomes from rolling two dice.

The probability, $P(n)$, of an outcome n, is the number of ways the outcome n can happen divided by the number of possible outcomes. We can write this probability as a function. The column labeled Probability Function describes the probability of getting the absolute value of the difference, n, when rolling two dice.

    d. Complete the Probability Function column.

    e. What is the sum of the entries in the Probability Function column?

    f. Graph $(n, P(n))$.

Section 3.0 Basic Operations on Polynomials

Preparation **Objectives**
- Identify a polynomial and types of polynomials.
- Add and subtract polynomials.
- Multiply monomials, binomials, and trinomials.
- Factor trinomials.
- Find common monomial factors.

Links
- Solving quadratic equations: Section 3.3.
- Completing the square with tables: Section 3.4.
- Special products and factoring cubic expressions: Section 4.0.
- Building quadratic equations with *x*-intercepts: Section 4.1.
- Finding the vertex of a parabola: Section 4.4.
- Simplifying and operating with rational expressions: Sections 5.3, 5.4, 5.5, and 5.6.
- Binomial Theorem: Appendix 3.

Time and Emphasis
50 minutes. Essential material.

Vocabulary

binomial	common monomial	factor
greatest common factor	prime number monomial	polynomial
prime factor	proof	trinomial

Points to Stress
- To factor expressions, use the problem-solving strategies *make a systematic list* and *guess and check*.
- The table method gives us a visual approach to the master-product/factor-by-grouping form of factoring. We use the table method for multiplying, factoring, completing the square, and factoring cubic expressions.
- Review of polynomials and their operations.
- Identify the types of polynomials, and identify which are polynomial expressions and which are not.
- Add, subtract, and multiply polynomials.
- Review factoring of monomials and trinomials.

Suggested Lesson Format
Warm-up: 5 minutes
Lecture/Group Activity: 40 minutes
Coaching for Homework: 5 minutes

Materials Needed for Class
Copies of *Polynomial Practice* (IRM page 53).

Optional: 3×5 cards for *Factoring Bee** game (IRM page 52).

Homework
Core exercises: 1 to 5, odd; 9 to 79, at least one exercise from each section.

Sample assignment: Exercises 1 to 78, every third exercise; problems 83, 85, and 87 (these are very good discussion problems).

> **For Labs and Recitations**
> Assign the project Powers of Binomials in Exercise 97.

---

*Thanks to Dr. Jolene Rhodes of Valencia Community College in Orlando, FL for the *Factoring Bee* game.

In Class **Warm-up**

(5 minutes): Assign the Warm-up to be done in groups or individually.

> *Journal Entry*
> After the students do this Warm-up, I demonstrate that exactly half of the factors of any number are found between 1 and the square root of the number to be factored. The students find this a fascinating way to factor large numbers. This is also a good time to review prime factorization.
> —LM-M

Lecture/Group Activity

(40 minutes): Polynomials. Begin with the definition of a polynomial. Use Example 1, which has polynomials and non-polynomials to review the definition. Do Examples 2 and 3 to review adding, subtracting, and multiplying polynomials. Conclude with factoring monomials out of polynomials and factoring trinomials, covered in Examples 10, 11, and 12. (The lists below have additional practice polynomials if you want to use them..) Introducing the table method of factoring gives students one last chance to become proficient at factoring trinomials. Group activity. Assign *Polynomial Practice* to be done individually and checked in groups. Optional activity. If times allows, and you think the students could use more practice, use the lists below to play *Factoring Bee* (below).

Coaching for Homework

(5 minutes): *For more practice in factoring, go to the Selected Answers, page 664, and factor the answers to Exercises 21 to 39, odd.*

Easy Trinomials with Binomial Factors	Slightly Challenging Trinomials with Binomial Factors	Binomial Squares
$x^2 + 7x + 10$	$2x^2 + 3x + 1$	$x^2 + 2x + 1$
$x^2 + 15x + 54$	$2x^2 + 5x + 2$	$x^2 + 4x + 4$
$x^2 + 8x + 15$	$2x^2 + 8x + 6$	$x^2 + 6x + 9$
$x^2 + 11x + 28$	$2x^2 + 7x + 3$	$4x^2 + 4x + 1$
$x^2 + 9x + 18$	$6x^2 + 15x + 6$	$9x^2 + 12x + 4$
$x^2 + 9x + 8$	$3x^2 + 7x + 2$	$x^2 + 10x + 25$
$x^2 + 9x + 20$	$3x^2 + 5x + 2$	$16x^2 + 8x + 1$
$x^2 + 10x + 21$	$3x^2 + 4x + 1$	
$x^2 + 5x + 6$	$6x^2 + 13x + 6$	
$x^2 + 6x + 8$	$6x^2 + 7x + 1$	

Special Products	Trinomials with Binomial Factors		Some Interesting Binomials
$x^2 - 2x + 1$	$2x^2 - 5x - 3$	$3x^2 \pm 2x - 1$	$x^2 - 1$
$x^2 - 4x + 4$	$2x^2 - 3x - 2$	$3x^2 \pm 5x - 2$	$x^2 - 4$
$x^2 - 6x + 9$	$2x^2 - x - 1$	$3x^2 \pm 8x - 3$	$4x^2 - 1$
$4x^2 - 4x + 1$	$2x^2 + 7x - 4$	$3x^2 - 8x + 4$	$2x^2 - 2$
$4x^2 - 25$	$12x^2 + 7x - 12$	$3x^2 - 4x + 1$	$3x^2 - 3$
$9x^2 - 16$	$6x^2 + 5x - 1$	$3x^2 - 8x + 5$	$-x^2 + 1$ (tricky, but not too tricky)
$4x^2 \pm 12x + 9$	$x^2 - x - 6$	$x^2 - 4x - 21$	
	$x^2 + 4x - 21$	$x^2 - 8x + 15$	
	$x^2 + 3x - 54$	$x^2 + 3x - 10$	

Factoring Bee
- The instructor provides a member of the first team with a factoring problem on a 3-by-5 card. The student writes the problem on the board and then has a specified time limit to factor the problem.
- If the student gets the problem correct, the first team receives 1 point and a member of the second team receives a new problem. If the student from the first team can not factor it or factors it incorrectly, the same problem is given to a member of the second team who then tries to factor it.
- This continues throughout the groups until the preset time limit for the game expires. The team with the most points is declared the winner.

Polynomial Practice

1.   Multiply the following expressions. You may use the table method if you wish.

       a. $(x-5)(x+7)$

       b. $(2x+1)(x-8)$

       c. $(3x-10)(2x-4)$

2.   Factor the following polynomials making sure to factor out the greatest common factor (if there is one) first. You may then use the table method if you wish.

       1. $x^2+7x+12$

       2. $y^2+3y-28$

       3. $6p^2+11p-10$

       4. $10x^2+4x-6$

       5. $2x^2+8x-24$

Section 3.1 The Square Root Function and the Pythagorean Theorem

Preparation

Objectives

- Explain the difference between square roots and principal square roots.
- Identify a square root function and its domain and range.
- Simplify expressions containing square roots.
- Apply the Pythagorean theorem when appropriate.

Links

- Solving quadratic equations: Section 3.3.
- Square roots of negative numbers: Section 4.3.
- Simplifying and operating with radical expressions: Sections 6.2, 6.3, and 6.4.

Time and Emphasis

50 minutes. Essential material.

Vocabulary

converse of the Pythagorean theorem	equilateral triangle	height of a triangle (altitude)
hypotenuse	isosceles right triangle	leg
plus or minus sign	principal square root	product property of square roots
radical sign	radicand	square root
square root function	vertex (of a triangle)	

Points to Stress

- Introduce the square root as a function and discuss its domain.
- Explain the difference between square roots and the principal square root as it arises when solving equations.
- Introduce the Pythagorean theorem and give examples (both symbolic and practical) of its uses.

Suggested Lesson Format

Warm-up: 5 minutes

Lecture/Group Activity: 35 minutes

Coaching for Homework: 5 minutes

Materials Needed for Class

Calculator for overhead projector

Rulers

Homework

<u>Core exercises</u>: 31 to 49, odd; 53 to 71, odd

<u>Sample assignment</u>: 1 to 71, odd; 75, 77, 83, 85. Students continuing on to courses containing trigonometry need to pay close attention to Examples 13, 14, and 15, and Exercises 75 to 87.

TIP

For electronics students, point out the similarities between the Pythagorean theorem and formula used for alternating current circuits:

$$(\text{impedance})^2 = (\text{resistance})^2 + (\text{reactance})^2$$

For Labs and Recitations

Review Examples 4 and 5. Compare the calculator results when a student fails to place parentheses around the expression in the numerator. Discuss why the 4s in Exercise 49 simplify to 1 and yet the 4s in Exercise 48 do not. [Answer: The 4 and $\sqrt{8}$ in Exercise 49 are factors while the 4 and $\sqrt{8}$ in Exercise 48 are terms not common factors. In Exercise 48 we must first simplify $\sqrt{8}$ to $2\sqrt{2}$ and then divide the numerator and denominator by 2 in order to simplify.]

Assign *Estimating and Simplifying Square Root Expressions* (IRM page 56).

Journal Entry I encourage my students to recite the squares of the numbers 1 to 16, 20, 25, and 30 at each stoplight or stop sign to and from school. This will help them learn squares and square roots. —AK

In Class   **Warm-up**

(5 minutes): Assign the Warm-up to be done in groups or individually. This is a good time to talk about squares and square roots of numbers greater than one compared to and square roots of numbers between zero and one.

Lecture/Group Activity

(35 minutes): Square roots. Review some of the properties of square roots covered in Examples 1, 3, and 5. Ask the students to compare the square roots of 1.44, 144, and 14,400: *Why isn't 1,440 included in this list?*

> **NOTE**
> In this chapter we are work informally with square roots, letting the students discover some of the properties through patterns, such as finding the square roots of 1.44, 144, and 14,400.
> We will formalize these properties when we simplify expressions in Chapter 6.

More about square roots: Demonstrate how to solve equations of the form $n^2 = c$. This is also a good time to demonstrate the solutions on a calculator graphically. A graph is a good way to convince students that equations like $x^2 = 4$ have two solutions.

The Pythagorean theorem. Introduce the Pythagorean theorem by having students work in groups on the exploration in Example 7. This is also a good time to get out rulers, have the students create their own right triangle, and verify that the Pythagorean theorem works for their triangle. Have the students create a non-right triangle and see if the Pythagorean theorem works for non-right triangles.

Do Example 8 with the class to show how to find a missing leg or missing hypotenuse in a right triangle. For practice finding missing sides of a right triangle, have the students work in groups on Exercise 54.

> **Journal Entry**
> Students often misunderstand the Pythagorean theorem to mean $a + b = c$. I use the following activity to help them discover why this cannot be true:
> After I introduce the Pythagorean theorem, I give each student two strips of paper of equal lengths. I ask the students to label one piece of paper c.
> Then I ask them to tear the second piece of paper into two pieces of unequal lengths and label the pieces a and b respectively. Then I ask them to create a triangle by connecting the ends of the paper strips.
> The students quickly discover that if $a + b = c$ no triangle can be formed!
> —LM-M

Applications of the Pythagorean theorem. Conclude the lesson by Example 12 with the class. This leaves the students with a practical application of the theorem.

Coaching for Homework: Discuss with students how they might solve Exercises 57 to 66. Point out that they did this in Example 7 in class.

Calculator note for Exercises 37 to 50: *Some calculators place a parentheses immediately after a square root sign. If no closing parenthesis is entered, the calculator assumes the closing parenthesis is at the end of the entire expression. Thus in Exercise 39, $\sqrt{5}$ becomes $1 - \sqrt{\dfrac{3}{2}}$. It needs to be entered $(1- \sqrt{} (3))/2$.*

After doing Exercise 75, look for a shortcut for doing 76 to 80 and another from Exercise 83 for doing 84 to 86. Your shortcut will avoid using the Pythagorean theorem each time. [Answers: In Exercises 75 to 80, the hypotenuse is $\sqrt{2}$ times the given side. In Exercises 83 to 86, the height is $\sqrt{3}$ multiplied by half the given side.]

> FUN ALERT Special Patterns Investigate the pattern formed by the squares of the numbers ending in 5. The pattern: The last two digits in the square of the digits $n5$ are 25. The product $n(n + 1)$ gives the number(s) in front.
> Thus 65^2 begins with $6 \cdot 7 = 42$ and ends with 25, 4225.

Estimating and Simplifying Square Root Expressions

Between what two integers is each square root expression?   For example, $2 < \sqrt{5} < 3$

1. $\_ < \sqrt{50} < \_$ 2. $\_ < \sqrt{20} < \_$ 3. $\_ < \sqrt{12} < \_$

4. $\_ < \sqrt{8} < \_$ 5. $\_ < \sqrt{18} < \_$ 6. $\_ < \sqrt{32} < \_$

Write an estimate of the value of each expression below.

$$\frac{a + \sqrt{b}}{c} = \frac{a}{c} + \frac{\sqrt{b}}{c}$$

Rewrite each expression using   . Simplify.
Evaluate your expression with a calculator. Compare with your original estimate.

Expression	Estimate	Rewrite and Simplify	Calculate
7. $\dfrac{2 + \sqrt{8}}{4}$			
8. $\dfrac{2 + \sqrt{32}}{4}$			
9. $\dfrac{2 - \sqrt{12}}{6}$			
10. $\dfrac{6 + \sqrt{8}}{3}$			
11. $\dfrac{2 + \sqrt{12}}{2}$			
12. $\dfrac{4 - \sqrt{8}}{2}$			
13. $\dfrac{4 - \sqrt{20}}{2}$			
14. $\dfrac{6 - \sqrt{18}}{3}$			
15. $\dfrac{3 - \sqrt{18}}{6}$			
16. $\dfrac{5 + \sqrt{50}}{5}$			
17. $\dfrac{5 - \sqrt{20}}{10}$			

Section 3.2 Quadratic Functions and Solving Quadratic Equations with Tables and Graphs

Preparation   **Objectives**
- Identify a quadratic function by number pattern.
- Identify a quadratic function from the equation form.
- Identify the input variable as well as coefficients a, b, and c in quadratic equations.
- Graph quadratic functions and find the domain and range.
- Find the intercepts, vertex, and axis of symmetry from a graph.
- Solve a quadratic equation with table or graph.

Links
- Patterns and sequences: Section 1.1, 2.4, and 7.0.
- Graphing: Section 1.2.
- Functions: Section 2.1.
- Degree of a polynomial: Section 4.0.
- Modeling quadratic functions: Section 4.1.
- Solving equations with tables and graphs: Sections 1.2, 2.0, 4.0, 5.6, 7.1, 8.1, and 8.5.

Time and Emphasis
50 minutes. Essential material.

Vocabulary

axis (line) of symmetry	cubic function	degree of a polynomial of one variable
first differences	parabola	quadratic function
quadratic sequence	second differences	vertex (of a parabola)
vertical motion equation	x-intercept points	y-intercept point

Points to Stress
- When given a function listed as a sequence, common second differences? distinguish quadratic functions from linear and other functions.
- Look carefully at units on the axes. The graph for vertical motion is often misinterpreted as the path of the dive. Digital clocks might be used to label the horizontal axis and tape measures for the vertical axis, page 188. When the graph shows the path of parabolic motion, consider drawing tape measures on both axes, page 264.

Suggested Lesson Format
Warm-up: 5 minutes
Questions on Homework: 10 minutes
Lecture/Group Activity: 25 minutes
Coaching for Homework: 5 minutes

Materials Needed for Class
None

Homework
Core exercises: 1 to 9, odd; 15 to 21, odd.
Sample assignment: 1 to 25, odd; 33, and 35.

For Labs and Recitations
CBL and Dropped Book. Gather data on a dropped book with the Texas Instruments CBL (Calculator Based Laboratory) and a motion sensor, as suggested in CBL Experiment Workbook Activity M2, *What Goes Up Must Come Down*. Add these questions to the student activity report:
  a. Describe the book-drop experiment.
  b. What are the units on the input for the experiment? the output? [Answers: time, height]
  c. What does $\frac{\Delta x}{\Delta y}$ mean in this setting? [Answer: velocity]
  d. Graph the data.
Return to this data when you do Section 4.1 and fit a quadratic equation.

In Class **Warm-up**

(5 minutes): Assign the following Warm-up to be done in groups.

1. Write these sequences. Have students use differences to find six other numbers in the output sequence as indicated by the blanks and answer the question that follows.

   a.   ___, ___, ___, 0, 0, 2, 6, 12, ___, ___, ___

   b.   ___, ___, ___, 4, 3, 0, −5, ___, ___, ___

2. How do these sequences compare with the linear sequences of Chapter 2?

Questions on Homework

(10 minutes): Have the students go over the homework in groups and select questions for class discussion.

Lecture/Group Activity

(25 minutes): Sequences and functions. Have the students work in groups on the explorations in Examples 1 and 2.

Define degree of a polynomial and quadratic functions. Refer back to the Warm-up: *Are the sequences in the Warm-up also quadratic?* Have students compare their results with Table 5 and Figure 20 (textbook page 183) and Table 7 and Figure 24 (textbook page 185). In Section 4.1, we will find equations from data.

Discuss the coefficients a, b, and c on a quadratic function, and identify a, b, and c on the sequences discussed thus far (or have students do Example 4).

Graphing quadratic functions. Begin this discussion with the question: *What is it about the data for quadratic equations that helps with the graphing?* Review x-intercept points, y-intercept point, and introduce axis (or line) of symmetry and vertex..

How are the graphs of the data (Figures 20 and 24) *from the Warm-up alike? How are they different?*[Answer: Both form parabolas. The parabola in Figure 20 turns up, that in Figure 24 turns down.]

Domain and range. Do Example 9 with the class.

Solving equations from tables and graphs. Do Example 11 with the class. Emphasize that Figure 26 shows the path of the dive (almost vertical) while the graph shows position or height for various times.

Coaching for Homework

(5 minutes): *In Part* j *of Exercise 19, factor out the −1 first.*

In Exercise 22, using r *as 0 to 20 in steps of 1 gives interesting, but incorrect, results; the correct evaluation is 0 to 0.20 in steps of 0.01.*

Section 3.3 Solving Quadratic Equations with Factors and Square Roots

Preparation

Objectives
- Solve a quadratic equation by factoring.
- Find x-intercepts by factoring.
- Apply absolute value in taking square roots.
- Solve linear absolute value equations.
- Solve a quadratic equation by taking the square root.
- Find x-intercepts for $y = ax^2 + c$ with square roots.
- Solve a formula with squares and square roots.

Links
- Factoring: Section 3.0.
- Square roots: Section 6.2, 6.3, and 6.4.
- Absolute value: Section 1.0, 2.4, and 6.2.

Time and Emphasis
50 minutes. Essential material.

Vocabulary

absolute value   quotient property of   zero product rule
                                square roots

Points to Stress
- The zero product rule applies to $(ax + b)(cx + d) = 0$ not $(ax + b)(cx + d) = 4$, or any other non-zero number.
- The zero product rule uses the phrasing *either/or* not *and*.
- The graph of $y = \sqrt{x^2}$ is the absolute value graph. The absolute value is why there are two solutions to $x^2 = c$ when we take the square root. The two solutions do not come from square root symbol (the principal square root).
- We can omit absolute values when taking square roots of formulas in which variables are defined only for positive real numbers.

Suggested Lesson Format
Warm-up: 5 minutes
Questions on Homework: 10 minutes
Lecture/Group Activity: 25 minutes
Coaching for Homework: 5 minutes

Materials Needed for Class
None

Homework
Core exercises: 1 to 31, odd; 35 to 39, odd; 47, 49; 53 to 59, odd; 69, 71, and 73.
Sample assignment: 1 to 73, odd.

For Labs and Recitations
To practice solving equations, do Example 4 and the project in Exercise 75 in groups.
   To practice simplifying expressions, assign Exercises 63 to 68 to be done in groups.

In Class

Warm-up

(5 minutes): Assign the Warm-up to be done individually and checked in groups. Point out that each of these problems is an expression not an equation. It is important that the students understand that this section is concerned with solving equations that have these expressions in them. Use the problems from the Warm-up when solving equations using the zero product rule.

Questions on Homework

(10 minutes): Have the students check the homework in groups and select questions for class discussion.

Lecture/Group Activity

(25 minutes): Place this section in context with other sections by discussing the summary on page 195.

Solving equations by factoring. Introduce the zero product rule. Have students do Examples 1 and 2.

Do Example 3 with the class: *Example 3 reminds us to set the factors equal to zero and solve the factor equations. Avoid the common error of simply taking the opposite of the number in the factor.*

True or false: If $A \cdot B = 10$ then is it always true that either $A = 10$ or $B = 10$? [Answers. Not necessarily. $A = 2$ and $B = 5$ make $A \cdot B = 10$ true but neither equal 10.] Discuss the most common error in applying the zero product rule, which is using factors to solve $A \cdot B = n$, a non-zero number. We must change the equation to the form $= 0$ before applying the zero product rule.

Absolute value and square roots. Have the students do Example 6. Formally define *absolute value*. Have students do Example 9 with a graph.

Solving quadratic equations by taking square roots. Mention the quotient property of square roots, page 203. Have the students do Example 11 and then Exercises 6 and 8 both by factoring and by taking square roots.

Coaching for Homework

Read Examples 12 and 13 before doing Exercises 41, 69, 73, or 74.

Section 3.4 Solving Quadratic Equations with the Quadratic Formula

Preparation

Objectives
- Identify squares of binomials.
- Use completing the square to form the squares of binomials.
- Derive the quadratic formula form $ax^2 + bx + c = 0$.
- Use the quadratic formula to solve equations.
- Use a calculator or solve program to solve quadratic equations.

Links
- Multiplying and factoring tables: Sections 3.0 and 4.0, and Appendix 3 (Binomial theorem).
- Completing the square: Section 4.4.
- Minimum and maximum: Section 4.5 (Based on the quadratic formula, not completing the square).
- Radical expressions: Section 6.3.

> **NOTE**
> During lesson planning, notice how the Warm-up problems tie in with the examples and explanations: Exercises 2 and 3 are repeated in Example 1; Exercises 10 and 6 are repeated in Example 3; and Exercise 6 is the transition between Step 3 and Step 4 of Example 5.

Time and Emphasis
50 minutes. Essential material.

Vocabulary

binomial square	completing the square	cross multiplication property
golden rectangle	perfect square trinomial	proportion
quadratic formula	ratio	

> *Journal Entry*
> I like to point out that the techniques I am about to introduce *always* work!
>   This is a good selling point for the quadratic formula!   —LM-M

Points to Stress
- Not every quadratic equation is easily factored to use the zero product rule; consequently, other techniques are required.
- Completing the square is a tool used here to derive the quadratic formula.
- We can use the quadratic formula to solve any equation.
- Most other methods, listed on page 195, are limited to special cases
- Equations must be placed into proper form in order to use the quadratic formula.

Suggested Lesson Format
Warm-up: 10 minutes
Questions on Homework: 10 minutes
Lecture/Group Activity: 25 minutes
Coaching for Homework: 5 minutes

Materials Needed for Class
None

Homework
Core exercises: 1 to 35, odd; 49 to 61, odd.
Sample assignment: 1 to 63, odd.

> Avoiding the Pitfalls
> If students need practice understanding polynomial expressions have them use algebra tiles to build squares from expressions, such as $x^2 + 2x + 1$, and $x^2 + 4x + 4$. See the list of polynomials for *Factoring Bee* (IRM page 000) for expressions that can be shown with algebra tiles.
>   Then have them practice completing the square with algebra tiles: $x^2 + 6x + \_\_$ and $a^2 + 2ab + \_\_$.

> **For Labs and Recitations**
> Here are two different activities to choose from:
> Do the project in Exercise 71 if you wish students to investigate solving equations of the quadratic form.
>   Help students program the quadratic formula into their calculators. Encourage them to use the quadratic formula program as a model for their own programs for finding slope, finding the distance between two points, and other common formulas.

In Class

Warm-up

(10 minutes): Assign the Warm-up to be done in groups. Ask the groups to explain how they did the last three exercises in the Warm-up. Use this to review squaring binomials.

Questions on Homework

(10 minutes): Have the students go over the homework in groups and select questions for class discussion.

> **TIP**
> If the students can derive the quadratic formula, modeling their work after the steps given in Example 5, they will be able to use the formula more effectively and understand the material. It is worth giving 5 points extra credit for successful derivations.

Lecture/Group Activity

(25 minutes): Completing the square. Discuss Figure 37, which shows the transition from the table method of multiplication to an area model for completing the square.

Assign the exploration in Example 1 to be done in groups. Review the definition of completing the square at the top of textbook page 209.

Have the students practice completing the square by doing Examples 2 and 3 in groups.

> **NOTE**
> We use the area model of binomial multiplication to emphasize the square in completing the square.
> With the area model, completing the square becomes a process of finding what needs to be written in the lower right corner to build a square.
> The visual learner needs to connect the square to completing the square. Symbolic thinkers are quite happy with the procedure box on page 210.

The quadratic formula. In order to derive the quadratic formula, it is useful to solve one equation by completing the square, such as Example 4, then present the general derivation in Example 5 in a parallel format. Steps 1 to 4 in the summary of completing the square describe the first 4 steps in deriving the quadratic formula. Stress that the quadratic formula is not complete without the statement $ax^2 + bx + c = 0$.

Using the quadratic formula. Assign Example 6 to be done in groups for practice in using the quadratic formula. Emphasize that the equation must be solved for zero in order to find the values of a, b, and c to apply the quadratic formula.

> **NOTE** Graphing Calculator
> The replay feature on the graphing calculator is useful in calculating the second solution to a quadratic equation once the first solution has been entered. Just replay and change the addition sign to a subtraction sign in front of the square root. A sample program for evaluating the quadratic formula is given on textbook page 216.

Graphical implications.
Do Example 7 with the class to lay the groundwork for imaginary numbers and to reinforce the number of possible solutions by comparing the graphs of quadratic equations.

Coaching for Homework

Exercises 37 to 42 practice identifying a, b, and c within formulas.

You may need to multiply binomial expressions in order to change to the standard form: $ax^2 + bx + c = 0$.

The values of a, b, and c have already been substituted into one part of the quadratic formula in Exercises 43 to 48. You are to find the original equation and then simplify the given expression without a calculator. The radical expressions all contain perfect squares.

Optional Activity

The Golden Ratio: The Golden Rectangle (textbook pages 214 to 216) gives an artistic application to quadratic equations and provides a nice balance to all the physics and engineering applications of algebra.

The Fibonacci sequence mentioned in Exercises 72 and 73 played an important role in the development of a new mathematical constant, described in Science News (Vol. 155, June 12, 1999, page 376). An excellent reference on Fibonacci numbers is H. E. Huntley's The Divine Proportion: A Study of Mathematical Beauty (New York: Dover Publications, 1970).

Section 3.5 Solving Quadratic Inequalities with Tables and Graphs

Preparation

Objectives
- Write inequalities in interval notation.
- Solve inequalities with a table or graph.
- Describe the solutions to quadratic inequalities relative to y-intercepts.
- Solve application problems involving inequalities.

Links
- Inequalities and graphs: Sections 1.0, 1.4, and 8.6.

Time and Emphasis
50 minutes. Essential material.

Vocabulary

infinite   infinity sign   interval

Points to Stress
- Intervals provide an important way to describe sets of numbers such as those needed to describe the inputs and outputs on the graphing calculator viewing window. They may be introduced informally prior to this section and then formalized here.
- Interval notation may look like an ordered pair. Read carefully when you see (a, b) to know whether the reference is to a coordinate point (a, b) or to an interval (a, b) describing the set $a < x < b$.
- Solving quadratic inequalities, $ax^2 + bx + c > 0$, starts out by finding the horizontal axis intercepts, just like solving quadratic equations, $ax^2 + bx + c = 0$.
- Identify the solutions by the relative position of the graph to the x-axis.

Suggested Lesson Format

Warm-up: 5 minutes

Questions on Homework: 15 minutes

Lecture/Group Activity: 20 minutes

Coaching for Homework: 5 minutes

Materials Needed for Class

None

Homework

Core exercises: 1 to 11, odd; 15 to 35, odd; 39 to 41, odd; 53 to 57.

Sample assignment: 1 to 41, odd; 53 to 59, odd.

> **For Labs and Recitations**
> Assign the project in Exercise 61, Distinguishing Intervals
> from Coordinates, do be done in groups.

In Class

Warm-up

(5 minutes): Assign the Warm-up to be done in groups.

Questions on Homework

(15 minutes): Have the students check the homework in groups and select a questions for class discussion.

> **NOTE**
> Planning note: the functions in Warm-up Exercise 1 is used in Example 4 and in Warm-up Exercise 4 is used in Example 3.

Lecture/Group Activity

(20 minutes): Intervals. Introduce interval notation and the infinity sign, then have the students work in groups to complete the table in Example 1.

Solving quadratic inequalities. Describe the emergency flare setting for Example 2 and have students work in groups on Examples 2 and 3. Remind them that the quadratic formula (used in Warm-up Exercise 3) will give the horizontal axis intercepts.

Remind students that any of the techniques for solving quadratic equations (summarized on textbook pages 233 and 234) may be used to find x-intercepts for either quadratic equations or inequalities.

Coaching for Homework

(5 minutes): *Example 6 returns to finding regions based on inequalities as introduced in Section 1.4 and extends the concepts from linear graphs to quadratic graphs. The example and related exercises, 53 to 58, are presented as matching problems.*

Section 4.0 Special Products of Binomials and Higher Order Polynomials and Their Graphs

Objectives

Preparation

- Factor perfect square trinomials.
- Factor differences of squares.
- Identify graphs related to squares of binomials and differences of squares.
- Factor sums and differences of cubes.
- Solve higher order polynomials with graphs.

Links

- Binomial squares: Sections 3.0, 3.4, 4.4, and Appendix 3
- Graphs of quadratic functions: Section 4.2
- Higher order equations: Section 4.3
- Completing the square: Section 4.4
- Rational expressions: Section 5.3
- Polynomial long division: Section 5.5

Time and Emphasis

50 minutes. Optional material. This section is required if you plan to emphasize completing the square in Section 4.4 or relating graphs to rational expressions and polynomial long division in Sections 5.3 and 5.5.

Vocabulary

binomial square	cubic expression	degree
difference of cubes	difference of squares	double root
general polynomial equation	horizontal shift	perfect square trinomial
square of a binomial	sum of cubes	vertical shift

Points to Stress

- When we change the factors $(a - b)(a - b)$ to $(a - b)^2$ we are emphasizing the square of the binomial or binomial square.
- The graphs associated with binomials squares, differences of squares, and sums and differences of cubes are unique and represent shifts of the graphs of $y = x^2$ and $y = x^3$.
- The intersections of the graphs with the x-axis can be used to write factors of the original expressions.

Suggested Lesson Format

Warm-up: 5 minutes

Questions on Homework: 10 minutes

Lecture/Group Activity: 25 minutes

Coaching for Homework: 5 minutes

Materials Needed for Class

Homework

Core exercises: 1 to 33, odd; 39 to 45, odd; 49.

Sample assignment: 1 to 49, odd; 57 to 67, odd.

For Labs and Recitations

Squares and Cubes Vocabulary Summary Chart (IRM page 67).

In Class

Warm-up

(5 minutes): Assign the Warm-up to be done individually.

Questions on Homework

(10 minutes): Have the students go over the homework in groups and select questions for class discussion.

Lecture/Group Activity

(25 minutes): Identifying squares of binomials and differences of squares. Define *squares of binomials* (they name the factored forms of binomials) and differences of squares (they name the product of multiplying a specific pair of binomials). Do Examples 1 and 4 as a class to practice identifying squares of binomials and differences of squares.

Solving equations with squares of binomials and differences of squares. Assign Examples 3, 5, and 6 to be done in groups.

Graphs of special products. Summarize the horizontal and vertical shifts in the graph of $y = x^2$ as found in the graphs of $y = $ *square of a binomial* and $y = $ *difference of squares*.

Sum of cubes and difference of cubes. Define the *sum of cubes* and the *difference of cubes*. Assign Examples 7 and 8 to be done in groups. Discuss the graphs in Example 8 in terms of shifts of $y = x^3$.

Stress how to use the tables to factor the sum or difference of cubes if the student remembers only the first factor, $a + b$ or $a - b$ as shown in Example 9.

Coaching for Homework

(5 minutes): *Exercises 18 to 24 may be answered with either fractions or decimals.*

Exercises 35 to 38, note that in the expression x - r, the constant r may be either a positive number or a negative number.

Example 10 and Exercises 61 to 69 review solving equations from a graph.

Squares and Cubes Summary Chart

The table below summarizes the names and algebraic expressions in Section 4.0.

a. Write three examples for each row under the Factors column using x and appropriate numbers.

b. Multiply out the expressions you write and enter the product in the Equivalent Product column. An example in variables a and b is given.

Factors	Equivalent Product
Binomial Square, also called Square of a Binomial $$(a + b)(a + b) = (a + b)^2$$	Perfect Square Trinomial $$a^2 + 2ab + b^2$$
Using the language of Section 4.3 these might be called a Conjugate Pair: $$(a - b)(a + b)$$	Difference of Squares $$a^2 - b^2$$
Cube of a Binomial $$(a + b)(a + b)(a + b) = (a + b)^3$$	Product of a Cube of a Binomial $$a^3 + 3a^2b + 3ab^2 + b^3$$
Factors $$(a - b)(a^2 + ab + b^2)$$	Difference of Cubes $$a^3 - b^3$$
Factors $$(a + b)(a^2 - ab + b^2)$$	Sum of Cubes $$a^3 + b^3$$

Section 4.1 Modeling Quadratic Functions

Preparation

Objectives
- Use x-intercepts and one other point to find a quadratic function.
- Use a table and differences to find a quadratic function.
- Use calculator regression to find a quadratic function.

Links
- Linear regression, Section 2.3.
- Arithmetic sequences: Section 2.4.
- x-intercepts and factors: Section 3.3.
- Quadratic sequences: Section 3.2.
- Exponential sequences and regression: Section 7.0.

Time and Emphasis

50 minutes. Optional material; essential if your course content includes sequences and regression (see Links, above)

Vocabulary

factor theorem   modeling functions   parameter
quadratic regression

Points to Stress
- To find a quadratic equation with x-intercepts x_1 and x_2 and one other point, use $y = a(x - x_1)(x - x_2)$.
- Use the difference method to find a, b, and c in $f(x) = ax^2 + bx + c$ from a quadratic sequence:
  1. List the sequence, and calculate the first and second differences.
  2. Find a, given that the constant second difference is $2a$.
  3. Work backwards from the second difference row to find c, the $f(0)$ term before the first term, $f(1)$.
  4. Use $f(1)$, $x = 1$, a, and c to find b in $f(x) = ax^2 + bx + c$.
- Use quadratic regression to fit a function to data if the data form a sequence with constant second differences or if the graph of the data has a parabolic or approximately parabolic shape.

Suggested Lesson Format

Warm-up: 5 minutes
Questions on Homework: 15 minutes
Lecture/Group Activity: 20 minutes
Coaching for Homework: 5 minutes

Materials Needed for Class

Homework

Core exercises: 1 to 15, odd; 19 to 32, odd.

Sample assignment: 1 to 33, odd.

Optional Activity Have groups find missing terms on the left of each sequence, then use regression to find the quadratic equation describing each sequence.

1. ___, ___, ___, 1, 4, 9, 16, …
2. ___, ___, ___, 2, 6, 12, 20, …
3. ___, ___, ___, 1, 3, 6, 10, 15, …
4. ___ , ___, ___, −1, 1, 7, 17, 31, …
5. ___, ___, ___, 4, −1, −8, −17, −28, …
6. ___, ___, ___, 0, −7, −20, −39, −64, …

> **For Labs and Recitations**
> Explore quadratic sequences found in a multiplication table from the Project in Exercise 35.

In Class **Warm-up**

(5 minutes): Assign the Warm-up to be done individually.

Questions on Homework

(15 minutes): Have the students go over the homework in groups and select questions for class discussion.

Lecture/Group Activity

(20 minutes): Building an equation from x-intercepts.

Warm-up Exercises 4 to 6 give quadratic expressions in factored form. Have the students work in groups to graph these expressions and identify the x-intercepts.

State the factor theorem and the factored form of the quadratic equation:

$y = a(x - x_1)(x - x_2)$.

Remind the students: *If an ordered pair lies on the graph of an equation, substituting that ordered pair into the equation makes a true statement.*

Have the students work in groups on Exercise 8 at the end of the section. Remind them to model the process shown in Example 1.

Building an equation from a sequence. We begin by finding a. Do Example 4 as a class, using the results from Examples 2 and 3 to find a in $y = ax^2 + bx + c$. Show how $f(0)$, the term prior to the first term of the sequence is c in $y = ax^2 + bx + c$.

Do Example 5 to find c for the sequence $-1, 1, 7, 17, 31, 49$.

Do Example 6 to find a and b for the same sequence. Summarize by having groups do Exercise 22, finding the equation for $4, 12, 24, 40, 60, ...$.

> **NOTE** For Class Discussion
>
> In Example 5, $f(0) = 1$ is larger than $f(1) = -1$. Why might this be true?
>
> Answer: Due to the symmetry of the graph of a quadratic function. The vertex of the graph for Example 5 has a vertex at $(1, -1)$. The points $(0, 1)$ and $(2, 1)$ are symmetric points on the graph.

Finding a quadratic equation with a calculator. Have the students work in groups to fit a quadratic regression to the data from Examples 3 and 5 using the steps in the Graphing Calculator Technique shown on page 259.

Coaching for Homework

(5 minutes):

The exercises suggest finding equations in two ways: with calculator regression and either the x-intercepts or quadratic sequences.

Exercises 5 to 16 refer to the quadratic equation in factored form:

$y = a(x - x_1)(x - x_2)$.

Section 4.2 The Role of *a*, *b*, and *c* in Graphing Quadratic Functions

Preparation

Objectives
- Determine the effect of a on the graph of $f(x) = ax^2$.
- Determine the effect of b on the graph of $f(x) = x^2 + bx$.
- Determine the effect of c on the graph of $f(x) = x^2 + c$

Links
- Graphs of a quadratic function: Section 3.2.
- Shape and position of quadratic graphs: Section 4.4.

Time and Emphasis

50 minutes. Optional material. More time may be needed depending on the calculator skills of the students.

Vocabulary

parameter

Points to Stress
- The role that *a* and *c* play in the quadratic function in the form of $f(x) = ax^2 + bx + c$.
- There are several forms we can use to write quadratic functions. The form $f(x) = ax^2 + bx + c$ is helpful for the quadratic formula more than for graphing.

Suggested Lesson Format

Warm-up: 5 minutes

Lecture/Group Activity: 40 minutes

Coaching for Homework: 5 minutes

Materials Needed for Class

Graph paper

Graphing calculators

Copies of *Quadratic Function Activity*, (IRM pages 59 to 61).

Homework

Core exercises: 5 to 23 odd; 27 and 29.

Sample assignment: 1 to 33, odd.

For Labs and Recitations

Do the project in Exercise 35 on vertex patterns.

In Class   **Warm-up**

(10 minutes): Assign Exercises 1 and 4 to be done individually and Exercises 2, 3, 5, 6 in groups. This Warm-up gives the students a good idea of how to enter values correctly in their calculators. For some students, it may be a surprise that $-x^2$ and $(-x)^2$ are different.

Lecture/Group Activity

(40 minutes): Have the students work on the Quadratic Function Activity in groups of two.

The concept of the impact a and c on the quadratic graph is an excellent place for students to do some discovery learning. Make certain the students remember what the *vertex* is. Also, they may need a reminder about the *axis of symmetry*. This activity is designed to reinforce several previously learned concepts, such as, domain, range, interval notation, equations of vertical lines and x and y intercepts.

This activity may take more than one class period to complete. Depending on the class, I usually ask the students to work on the rest of the activity at home and bring it in the next day. I then allow them about 15 to 20 minutes to compare answers with their partners.

When the students have completed the activity, I wrap up the session with the main concepts I wanted them to learn. Basically, I ask them to tell me what impact a and c have on the quadratic function. We might have a brief discussion about the b value, but the most important concepts are that a dictates the steepness and direction of the graph and c forms the y-intercept.

Coaching for Homework

(5 minutes): *In Exercises 33 and 34, the figure is the same as that in Example 6, but the origin has been moved. Draw a sketch of the figure on their assignment, indicating both the old and new origin positions.*

Quadratic Function Activity

<u>Materials needed</u>: Graph paper and a graphing calculator.

<u>Activity</u>: The purpose of this activity is to explore quadratic functions. These functions are written in the general form $y = ax^2 + bx + c$, where a, b, and c are constants similar to the constants in the linear function, $y = mx + b$.

Part 1

For each of the graphs below find the following:
  a. The x-intercepts (there could be one, two or none of these).
  b. The y-intercept (there should be only one; why is this?).
  c. The axis of symmetry (on the x-axis).
  d. The ordered pair that describes the vertex. (the highest or lowest point on the graph).
  e. The domain and range of the graph (assume that each graph continues in the direction shown by the arrows on the graph).

1. a. _____

   b. _____

   c. _____

   d. _____

   e. _____

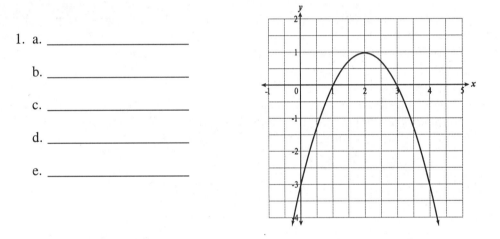

2. a. _____

   b. _____

   c. _____

   d. _____

   e. _____

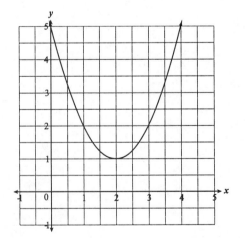

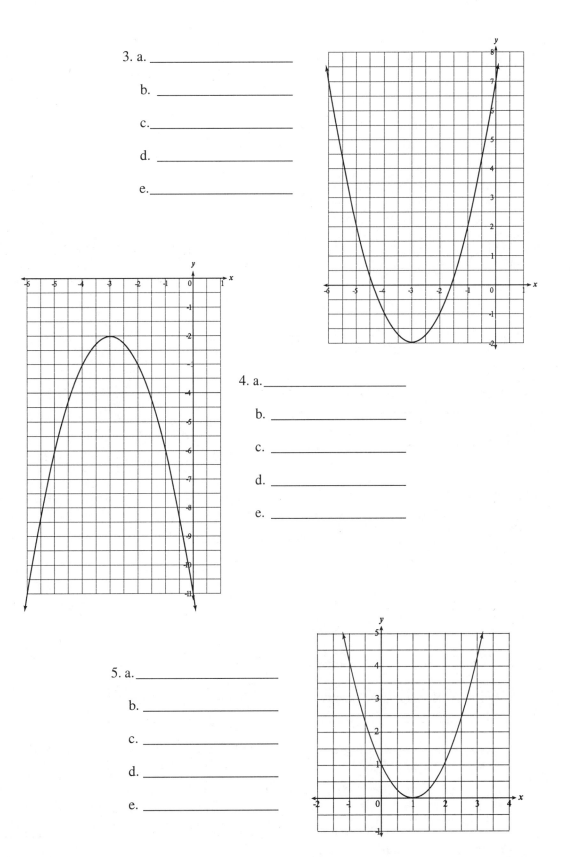

3. a. _____

   b. _____

   c. _____

   d. _____

   e. _____

4. a. _____

   b. _____

   c. _____

   d. _____

   e. _____

5. a. _____

   b. _____

   c. _____

   d. _____

   e. _____

6. Using complete sentences, explain the relationship between the axis of symmetry and the vertex..

7. Using complete sentences, explain the relationship between the vertex and the range of each function.

8. Using complete sentences describe the general shape of the graphs. (Are these functions? What is this shape called?)

Part 2

For each of the equations below, identify the values a, b, and c.

1. $f(x) = -x^2 + 4x - 3$ $a =$ $b =$ $c =$

2. $f(x) = (x - 2)^2 + 1$ $a =$ $b =$ $c =$ (Be careful!)

3. $f(x) = x^2 + 6x + 7$ $a =$ $b =$ $c =$

4. $f(x) = -x^2 - 6x - 11$ $a =$ $b =$ $c =$

5. $f(x) = (x - 1)^2$ $a =$ $b =$ $c =$ (Be careful!)

    a. If you graph each of the functions above, which graphs will open up?

    b. If you graph each of the functions above, which graphs will open down?

6. The functions listed in **Part 2** match the graphs in **Part 1**. How does the value of a impact each graph? (If you are unsure try graphing $y = x^2$ and $y + -x^2$. What do you notice?)

7. Compare the y-intercept of each graph in **Part 1** with the functions listed in **Part 2**. How does the value of c impact each graph?

Part 3

Let's investigate 'a' a little more carefully. Graph the following functions on the same axes.

1. $f(x) = x^2$

2. $f(x) = 2x^2$

3. $f(x) = -2x^2$

4. $f(x) = 0.5x^2$

5. $f(x) = 0.1x^2$

6. $f(x) = 4x^2$

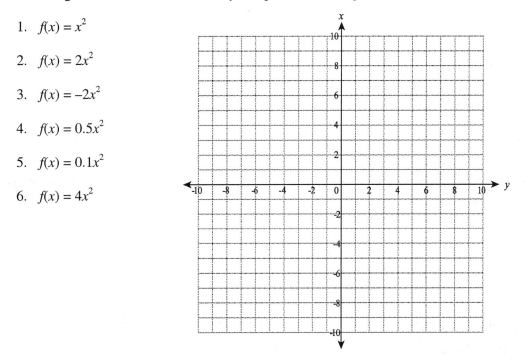

7. How would you modify your answer to Exercise 6 in Part 2 given what you have just graphed. Carefully explain the impact the constant a will have on any quadratic graph using as much detail as necessary.

8. Without actually graphing the function describe what the graph will look like for the following function (be sure to describe it so that someone without a calculator would know how to draw it!): $f(x) = -0.3x^2 + 6$.

Section 4.3 Complex Numbers and Graphs of Functions

Preparation

Objectives

- Use the discriminant, $b^2 - 4ac$, to identify the number and type of roots of quadratic equations.
- Change square roots of negative numbers into complex number notation.
- Identify complex conjugates.
- Add, subtract, and multiply complex numbers.
- Multiply and simplify binomials containing irrational and complex numbers.
- Write complex solutions to quadratic and other equations.

Links

- Quadratic formula: Section 3.4.
- Higher order expressions: Section 4.0.
- Polynomial long division: Section 5.5.

Time and Emphasis

50 minutes. Optional material.

Vocabulary

complex conjugate　　　complex number system　　　discriminant
imaginary unit

Points to Stress

- There are three different types of solutions for quadratic equations: two real numbers, one real number as a double root, or two complex numbers.
- Show solutions for quadratic equations graphically and algebraically with the discriminant.
- The degree of a polynomial equation indicates the maximum number of real-number solutions or the total number of real-number and complex-number solutions to $f(x) = 0$.
- The number of x-intercepts for a quadratic equation graph depends on the number and type of solutions to $f(x) = 0$.
- Only real numbers appear on a rectangular coordinate graph.
- If n is a positive number, then $\sqrt{-n} = i\sqrt{n}$, where i is the imaginary unit.
- Give definitions of addition, subtraction, and multiplication of complex numbers.
- Develop skills for simplifying expressions with imaginary numbers.

Suggested Lesson Format

Warm-up: 5 minutes
Lecture/Group Activity: 40 minutes
Coaching for Homework: 5 minutes

Materials Needed for Class

Graphing calculators
Transparency of coordinate grids (IRM page 78).

Homework

<u>Core exercises</u>: 1 to 17, odd.
<u>Sample assignment</u>: 1 to 73, odd.

For Labs and Recitations

Assign the Project on Complex Conjugates in Exercise 76. This shows how we might "divide" complex numbers. Application: By multiplying by i show that $\frac{1}{i} = -1$. This is a common substitution in electronics where RLC (resistance, inductance, capacitance) circuit equations contain the j-operator as the imaginary unit.

$$Z = R + \frac{1}{j\omega C} \text{ is the same as } Z = R - \frac{j}{\omega C}$$

$$Z = R + j\omega L + \frac{1}{j\omega C} \text{ is the same as } Z = R + j(\omega L) - \frac{1}{\omega C}.$$

The Project in Exercise 78 suggests investigating patterns in the powers of i.

In Class

Warm-up

(5 minutes): Assign the Warm-up to be done individually and checked as a class.

Lecture/Group Activity

(40 minutes): Motivating this section. Assign Example 1 to be done in groups to motivate this section

Solving functions graphically. Draw graphs of the following functions to review how to solve $f(x) = 0$ graphically:

$$f(x) = x^2 + 4x + 3, \quad f(x) = x^2 + 4x + 4, \text{ and } f(x) = x^2 + 4x + 5$$

After the students are convinced that each of these equations has different types of solutions, bring in the quadratic formula and introduce the concept of the sign of the discriminant.

Imaginary unit and complex numbers. Introduce the concept of i and how we use i to work with square roots containing negative numbers (see the definition boxes on pages 373 and 374.

Assign Examples 3 to be done in groups.

Return to the solutions to Warm-up Exercise 3 to introduce the concept of a complex number. Then have the students work on Examples 4 and 5 in groups.

Operations with complex numbers. Explain addition and subtraction with complex numbers (using the equations on page 275). Have the students work in groups on Example 6.

Explain how to multiply complex numbers, then have the students work on Example 7 in groups.

Solving equations with complex solutions. Do Examples 8 and 9 as a class. Then have the students work in groups to solve the following equations:

1. $x^2 + 2x + 3 = 0$ [Answer $x = -1 \pm -i\sqrt{2}$]
2. $x^2 + 2x - 3 = 0$ [Answer: $x = 1, -3$]
3. $x^3 - 8 = 0$ Hint: $x^3 - 8 = (x - 2)(x^2 + 2x + 4)$ [Answer: $x = 2, \ 1 \pm i\sqrt{3}$]

If time allows, do the rest of the exercises as a class. Remind the students that these are examples of proportionality and that cross multiplication works. Also, remind them that certain values are not allowed as possible solutions (meaningless replacements).

4. $\dfrac{1}{x+5} = \dfrac{x+5}{9}$ [Answer: $x \neq -5$; $x = -8, -2$]

5. $\dfrac{4}{x-1} = \dfrac{x+2}{10}$ [Answer: $x \neq 1$; $x = -7, 6$]

6. $\dfrac{x+1}{5} = \dfrac{-5}{2x-1}$ [Answer: $x \neq \dfrac{1}{2}$ $x = \dfrac{-1 \pm i\sqrt{191}}{4}$]

For closure, remind the students to look at the graphs of the equations 1, 2, and 3 that you have just solved algebraically. Having a picture

Coaching on Homework

(5 minutes): *Exercises 37 to 40 show several sets of complex factors for square numbers and prime numbers that do not appear in the real number system. The project on Rationalizing Denominators, Exercise 77, may be delayed until Section 6.3 and used at that time to motivate rationalization work with radicals.*

Avoiding the Pitfalls Make sure that students understand Exercise 3 of the warm-up. These skills are very weak in most students.

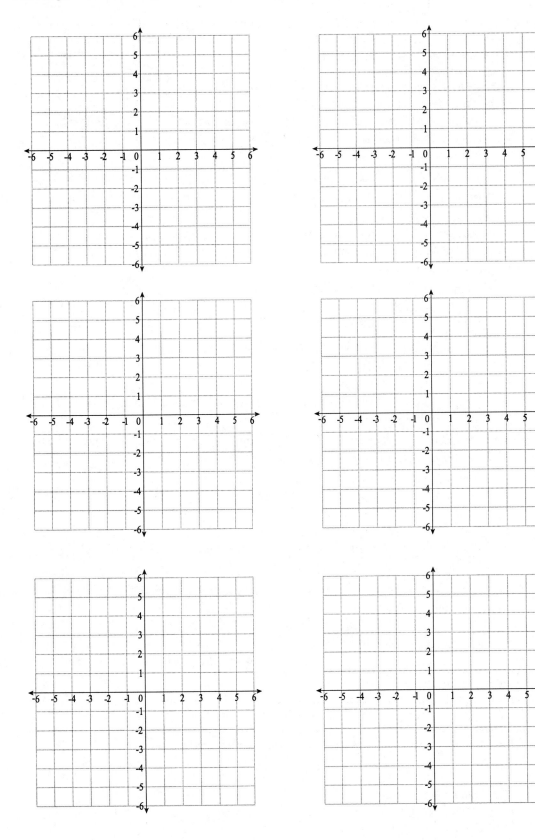

Section 4.4 Shifts, Vertex Form, and Applications of Quadratic Functions

Preparation

Objectives
- Identify horizontal or vertical shifts of $y = x^2$.
- Use the vertex form to predict the graph of a quadratic equation.
- Find the vertex from a quadratic equation in vertex form.
- Find the equation of a parabola from its vertex and one other point.
- Use completing the square to change a quadratic equation to vertex form.

Links
Binomial squares: Section 3.0, 4.0, and Appendix 3.
Quadratic graphs: Section 3.2.
Completing the square: Section 3.4.
Horizontal shifts: Section 4.0.
Exponential equations: 7.1.
Vertical shifts: Section 4.0, and 4.2.

Time and Emphasis
50 minutes. Essential material.
50 minutes. Optional material. Note that Section 4.5, Solving Minimum and Maximum Problems, does not depend on this section.

Vocabulary
horizontal shift   vertical shift   translation
vertex form of a quadratic equation

Points to Stress
- Given $f(x) = (x - h)^2 + k$ determine the impact of (h, k) on the quadratic graph as well as determine that this point forms the vertex of the parabola.
- Completing the square in order to change the general form of a quadratic to the vertex form.
- Determining the equation of a parabola given its vertex and a point

Suggested Lesson Format
Warm-up: 5 minutes
Lecture/Group Activity: 80 minutes
Coaching for Homework: 5 minutes
Note: The In Class lecture and group activity will take two days to complete.

Materials Needed for Class
Graphing calculator
Copies of *Shifty Functions* (IRM pages 81 to 83).

Homework
Core exercises: 1 to 21, odd.
Sample assignment: 1 to 41, odd.

For Labs and Recitations
Reinforce the horizontal and vertical shift concepts by examining absolute value functions as suggested in the project in Exercise 43.

In Class

Warm-up

(5 minutes): Do the Warm-up at the beginning of the section. Especially focus on Exercise 3 in the Warm-up.

Lecture/Group Activity

(80 minutes): Have students work in groups on the activity *Shifty Functions*. This is another excellent place for students to "discover" the properties of h and k in the quadratic form $f(x) = a(x -h)^2 + k$.

Note:

When the students have finished the activity, summarize their findings about the vertex as well as the vertical and horizontal shifts that the graphs experience.

Also, emphasize the fact that changing the a coefficient does not move the vertex. Recall what impact a has on the graph. Reminding the students about the various properties ($a < 0$, $|a| > 1$, and $|a| < 1$) helps to reinforce previous sections.

> **Avoiding the Pitfalls**
>
> Many students have difficulty with the "opposite" idea of $-h$. It is a good idea to check that they have gotten the idea down. To avoid overlooking this important point, the worksheet for *Shifty Functions* has instructions for the students to check with you when they have finished Exercise 1 in the activity.

At this point, it is helpful to bring in the idea of completing the square to get the function in the form $f(x) = a(x -h)^2 + k$ to locate the vertex. Have the students practice a few problems.

Remind the students that many real-life problems are modeled with parabolas. The equation of the path of objects can easily be determined if the vertex and another point of the path are known. Doing Exercises 31 and 34 in this section, help to give the students an idea of where parabolas are used. Many students love to watch basketball. Bring in a video of Michael Jordan (or some other good 3-point shooter) and have the students calculate the path of one of his shots. This is always a successful way to get the students to realize what information they need in order to find the equation of the path.

Wrap-up

Have the students graph the equations from Exercise 31 and/or 34 and write the equations in vertex form. Point out the placement of the vertex and the values for h and k in the equation. Remind the students that the vertex form helps with graphing the function and gives them the tool to locate the "peak" or maximum value for the path. This leads into the maximization problems in the next section.

Coaching for Homework

Exercises 53 to 42: Indicate whether or not completing the square to obtain the vertex form is optional. (See Section 4.5 for an alternative to completing the square to find the vertex.)

The students will find Exercises 29 to 34 the most challenging (probably due to the amount of words, not to the actual skills involved). Point out that they have worked out two of these problems in class.

Shifty Functions

The general form for a quadratic function is $f(x) = ax^2 + bx + c$. Another way to write a quadratic function is $y = (x - h)^2 + k$ or if we move k to the left side, we get $y - k = (x - h)^2$. To derive this new form of a quadratic function, we would use the completing the square method. We will not focus on arriving at this form. Rather, we will focus on what the constants h and k tell us about the graph.

1. Identify h and k in the following functions:
   a. $y = (x - 2)^2 - 4$ b. $y = (x + 3)^2 - 1$ c. $y - 5 = (x + 4)^2$ d. $y + 2 = (x - 3)^2$

Have the instructor check your work before moving on to Exercise 2.

2. Use your calculator to graph each of the functions in Exercise 1. Be sure to change Parts c and d to the form $y = (x - h)^2 + k$ by moving the k to the right side of the equation. Make sketches of the graphs below.

a.   b.

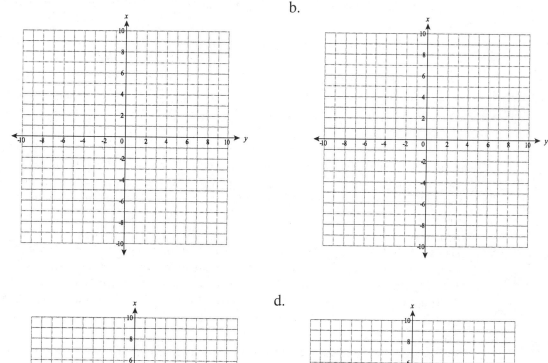

c.   d.

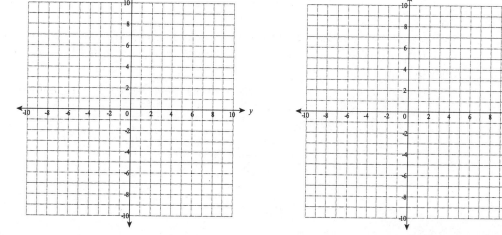

3. For each of the graphs in Exercise 2, identify the vertex.

   a.   b.   c.   d.

4. With your calculator set at the standard screen size, graph each of the following functions together. (Remember the order in which they are being graphed.) Make sketches of the graphs on the same axes. <u>Label each function</u>.

   a. $y = x^2$ b. $y = x^2 + 4$ c. $y = x^2 - 8$ d. $y = x^2 - 2$

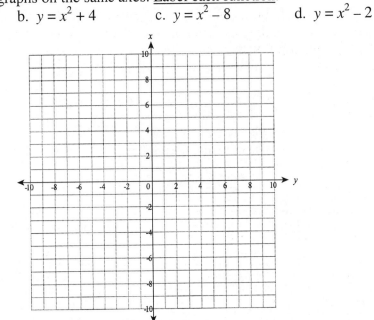

5. In a complete sentence or two, describe what effect k has on the graph. Notice that all of he functions in Exercise 4 are written in the form $y = (x - 0)^2 + k$.

6. On a new screen, graph all of the following functions. Make sketches of the graphs on the same axes. <u>Label the functions.</u>

   a. $y = x^2$ b. $y = (x - 2)^2$ c. $y = (x + 7)^2$ d. $y = (x + 4)^2$

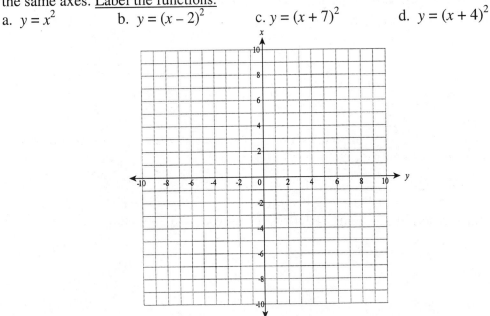

7. In a complete sentence or two, describe the effect that h has on the graph. Notice that all of the functions in Exercise 6 were written in the form $y - 0 = (x - h)^2$ or $y = (x - h)^2 + 0$.

8. Before using your calculator, make educated guesses about the shapes of these graphs. Identify h and k. Check your guesses on the calculator. (You may have to move k to the right side of the equation.) Sketch each graph on the same axes.

a. $y = (x - 3)^2 + 6$

b. $y = (x + 5)^2 - 4$

c. $y + 3 = (x - 6)^2$

d. $y - 6 = (x + 7)^2$

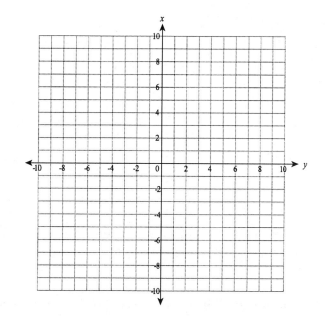

9. Identify the vertex in each of the parabolas in Exercise 8. In a sentence or two, explain how h and k relate to the vertex?

a.   b.

c.   d.

10. Graph $y = (x - 2)^2 + 6$ on your calculator. Notice what happens to the vertex if you change the value of a in $y = a(x - h)^2 + k$. Graph the following.

a. $y = 3(x - 2)^2 + 6$ b. $y = -3 (x - 2)^2 + 6$ c. $y = 0.3 (x - 2)^2 + 6$

Write a sentence describing what impact a has on the vertex of a parabola?

Section 4.5 Solving Minimum and Maximum Problems

Preparation

Objectives
- Find the vertex from the graph, intercepts, and quadratic formula.
- Solve minimum and maximum application problems.

Links
- Vertex: Sections 3.2 and 4.4.
- Quadratic formula: Section 3.4.
- Transition curves: Section 8.0.

Time and Emphasis
50 minutes. Essential material.
You may spend two days on this section and include the Optional Activity below.

Vocabulary

maximum   minimum x-coordinate of the vertex
y-coordinate of the vertex   transition curves

Points to Stress
- The x-coordinate of the vertex is the midpoint between the x-intercepts.
- The x-coordinate of the vertex is the midpoint of any horizontal segment that intersects the parabola in two points.
- For the function $f(x) = ax^2 + bx + c$, the x-coordinate of the vertex is the $-\dfrac{b}{2a}$ portion of the quadratic formula. The y-coordinate of the vertex is the output,

$$f(\frac{-b}{2a})$$

Suggested Lesson Format
Warm-up: 5 minutes
Questions on Homework: 10 minutes
Lecture/Group Activity: 25 minutes
Coaching for Homework: 5 minutes

Materials Needed for Class
None

Homework
Core exercises: 1 to 10, all.
Sample assignment: 1 to 10, all; 11, 13, and 19 to 29, odd.
For more practice, find the vertices in Exercises 35 to 42, Section 4.4, using x-coordinate of the vertex as $x = -\dfrac{b}{2a}$.

Optional Activity (on a second day)
CBL Activity Gather data on a tossed book with the Texas instruments Calculator Based Laboratory (CBL) and a motion sensor, as suggested by the CBL Experiment Workbook Activity M2, *What Goes Up Must Come Down.*
  a. Describe the book toss experiment.
  b. What units are on the input and output axes for a graph?
  c. What does the change in y divided by the change in x mean in the setting?
  d. Select data from those generated by the CBL, and fit a quadratic equation to the data.
  e. What other questions might we ask, or how might we vary the book toss experiment?

> **For Labs and Recitations**
> Do Exercises 15 and 16.

In Class

Warm-up

(5 minutes): Assign the Warm-up to be done individually.

Questions on Homework

(10 minutes): Have the students go over the homework in groups and select questions for class discussion.

Lecture/Group Activity

(25 minutes): Vertex. Have the students work in groups to sketch the graphs of the functions in Warm-up Exercises 1 to 4. *Show clearly the x-intercepts and the vertex from your graph.*

How is the x-coordinate of the vertex related to the x-intercepts?

[Answer: The x-coordinate of the vertex is the midpoint between the x-intercepts.]

How is the x-coordinate of the vertex related to special form of the quadratic formula statement you found in the Warm-up?

[Answer: The x-coordinate of the vertex is the $-\dfrac{b}{2a}$ portion of the quadratic formula.]

Applications Do Example 6 and Example 7 as a class.

NOTE Transition curves like those given in Example 7 and Exercises 23 to 28 are derived in Section 8.0.

Coaching for homework

(5 minutes):

In Exercises 11 to 22, state the appropriate formulas for each application.

In Exercises 23 to 26, the equations are provided. The accompanying data is provided to give a more complete setting. You will derive the equations in Chapter 8.

Avoiding the Pitfalls
For students who have difficulty visualizing that a square is a rectangle, suggest the project in Exercise 31.

Section 5.0 Rational Functions and Variation

Preparation

Objectives
- Identify rational numbers.
- Find equivalent rational numbers.
- Find the least common denominator.
- Perform operations with rational numbers.
- Simplify expressions containing units, and set up a unit analysis.

Links
- Units and Unit analysis: Sections 5.3 and 5.4.
- Rational expressions and equations: Sections 5.3, 5.4, and 5.6.
- Scientific notation: 6.0.

Time and Emphasis
50 minutes. This is essential material if unit analysis is not taught in the prerequisite course.

Vocabulary
equivalent fraction property	evaluate	least common denominator
rate	rational numbers	unit analysis

Points to Stress
- We review operations with fractions in this section to practice rational expressions, which will be needed later in the chapter.
- We introduce unit analysis to reinforce using units in applications.
- The logic in changing units in unit analysis is similar to the logic used in multiplying fractions and rational expressions.

> **NOTE** Operations with units are included with rational numbers because the student can relate to the simplifications with words where as the rational expressions may be more obscure. The simplification steps, particularly in multiplication, division, and complex fraction expressions, are parallel.

- The process of unit analysis formalizes what many students do mentally when they work through a problem. The process helps with more difficult problems.

Suggested Lesson Format
Warm-up: 5 minutes
Questions on Homework: 10 minutes
Lecture/Group Activity: 25 minutes
Coaching for Homework: 5 minutes

Materials Needed for Class
None

Homework Assignment
Core Exercises: 7 to 13, odd; 15 to 21, odd; 27 to 39, odd.
Sample Assignment: 1 to 53, odd.

> **For Labs and Recitations**
> Use the activity *Fractions and Unit Analysis* on IRM page 88.

In Class   **Warm-up**

(5 minutes): Assign the Warm-up to be done individually. Remind students that if they miss any of the warm-up problems, they should review pages 313 to 315. The remainder of the lesson focuses on units and unit analysis.

Questions on Homework

(10 minutes): Have the students go over the homework in groups and select questions for class discussion.

Lecture/Group Activity

(25 minutes): Changing from one unit to another. Remind the students that units may be simplified within a fraction or a product of fractions. Have the students do Example 6.

An example of changing units. One measure of airline service is the number of passenger • hours in delays for departure from airports. Suppose a Boeing 757 with 140 passengers leaves Chicago 40 minutes late. Calculate the number of passenger • hours in the delay.

> **NOTE** We use unit analysis for changing units and rates that are proportional. The most familiar exception to proportional units is the linear formula required for changing between Celsius and Fahrenheit,
>
> $C = \dfrac{5}{9}(F - 32)$.
>
> For more on proportional data versus non-proportional data, see Section 5.1, pages 329 to 331.

[Answer: $140 \text{ passengers} \bullet 40 \text{ minutes} \bullet \dfrac{1 \text{ hour}}{60 \text{ minutes}} = 93\dfrac{1}{3} \text{ passengers} \bullet \text{hours}$

This example shows how we can write a fact as a fraction and multiply to change units. This is the basic principle behind unit analysis.

To introduce unit analysis do Example 8 as a class. Then summarize with the box at the top of page 318, and have students do Example 9 in groups. Discuss the need to use facts twice to obtain square units and three times to obtain cubic units.

Rate-to-rate changes. To introduce rate-to-rate changes in unit analysis assign Example 10 to be done in groups. Then for practice problem solving and unit analysis, assign Example 11.

Coaching for Homework

Although the answers to some unit analyses may be written $\left(\dfrac{1 \text{ yard}}{3 \text{ feet}}\right)^3$ encourage

students to write the fraction as three separate factors, $\dfrac{1 \text{ yard}}{3 \text{ feet}} \bullet \dfrac{1 \text{ yard}}{3 \text{ feet}} \bullet \dfrac{1 \text{ yard}}{3 \text{ feet}}$ to

emphasize how the cubic units are formed.

The answer to the project in Exercise 65 will be in scientific notation. See Section 6.0 as needed.

For Labs and Recitations Unit Analysis with Fractions

Materials needed: Have each group fold one sheet of paper in half several times and tear along the folds until the resulting rectangles are approximately 2 inches by 2.5 inches.

Instructions: Have students list the facts that will be needed to solve a problem. The fact 5280 feet = 1 mile is needed in the problem below. Each group writes the pairs equivalent units on a rectangle of paper. They should write 5280 feet over 1 mile on the front and 1 mile over 5280 feet on the back. Each group needs one card for each fact.

Problem 1: You are driving 70 miles per hour. How many feet per second are you traveling?

[Answer: $102\frac{2}{3}$ feet per second.]

Problem 2: At 70 miles per hour, how many car lengths of spacing should you leave between you and a car ahead of you for a 3-second margin of safety? Suppose one car length is 20 feet.
[Answer: In 3-seconds the car travels 308 feet which is 15.4 car lengths.]

Problem 3: A child chasing a ball runs between parked cars and into the street exactly a half-block ahead of you. Suppose the block is 300 feet long.
  a. At 30 miles per hour, how many seconds will it take to reach the child's position?
    [Answer: ≈3.41 seconds]
  b. At 20 miles per hour (the speed limit), how many seconds will it take to reach the child's position?
    [Answer: ≈5.11 seconds]
  c. Extension: Comment on the benefits of driving the speed limit.
    [Answer: You have 50% longer to react and stop when traveling at 20 mph than 30 mph.]

Problem 4: Suppose the population of Chicago, Illinois is rounded to 3 million.
  a. If each person uses 123 gallons of water a day, how many gallons of water are used in a year? The answer will be in scientific notation.
    [Answer: 1.34685×10^{11} gallons]
  b. Change the gallons of water in part a to cubic feet. Hint: 1 gallon = 231 cubic inches
    [Answer: ≈1.8×19^{10} cubic feet.]
  c. Extension: What are the dimensions (in feet) of a cube big enough to hold this water?
    [Answer: The cube of ≈2621 feet on each side (about a half mile).]

Section 5.1 Ratios, Proportions, and Direct Variation

Preparation

Objectives
- Find when ratios are equal.
- Solve word problems and similar triangle problems with proportions.
- Find when linear data represent a direct variation.
- Translate word problems into linear, quadratic, or joint variation.

Links
Units: Section 5.0.
Linear equations: Sections 2.2, and 2.3.
Quadratic functions: Section 3.2.
Proportions: Section 5.6

Time and Emphasis
50 minutes. Essential material.

Vocabulary

constant of proportionality	constant of variation	corresponding angles
corresponding sides	cross multiplication property	
direct variation	equivalent ratios	joint variation
linear variation	proportion	quadratic variation
ratio	similar triangles	volume of a pyramid

Points to Stress
- All fractions are ratios.
- Two ratios are equal if they form a proportion.
- The use of proportions in geometry for similar triangles is important in many practical applications.
- Proportions can be linear, quadratic, joint or inverse (this last one is covered more thoroughly in the next section). These are very important concepts in many real-life applications.

Suggested Lesson Format
Warm-up: 5 minutes
Lecture/Group Activity: 40 minutes
Coaching for Homework: 5 minutes

Materials Needed for Class
If you have a model of similar triangles this is great to demonstrate that indeed the interior angles are the same. This is also a good time to remind the students of some geometric properties of triangles. I have them construct a paper triangle which they then tear off into three parts which each have one of the three angles. They put the angles together to actually "see" that the interior angles add to 180 degrees.

Homework
Core exercises: 1 to 16, odd.

Sample assignment: 1 to 63, every third exercise.

For Labs and Recitations

That students think all linear data is proportional is a common complaint from science instructors. Have students do Example 13 in pairs and then compare their results with the graphs, Example 14, to formulate a way to tell whether linear data varies directly.

In this section we show that proportionality depends on the graph of the linear data passing through the origin, giving a visual meaning to constant variation, $y/x = k$. When linear data is proportional we say it varies directly. In this case the ratio of the data points (x, y) is constant: $y/x = k$.

In Class

Warm-up

(5 minutes): Assign the Warm-up to be done individually. This is good for practice with fractions. Ask the students to try these problems without using their calculators.

Lecture/Group Activity

Similar triangles. After reminding the students about properties of triangles, I give them a similar triangle problem and ask the students to find the missing sides. (This could be a problem like Exercise 16.) This is a good time to talk about properties of triangles. I sometimes give out the "bonus point" problem of finding the height of a tree in their neighborhood using shadow lengths. I make it clear

> *Journal Entry* Because there are so many different ideas in this section, I have found it easiest to demonstrate a concept then let the students try one. At first, we start with the review of operations on fractions as well as when to use cross-multiplication.   —L M-M

that the tree must be over 20 ft tall. (Of course, this is a tough assignment in the Pacific Northwest where the sun is rarely out long enough to calculate the length of a tree's shadow!)

Proportions. We move to Example 10, which I do for the class, mentioning that this forms a linear proportional relationship. I emphasize that proportionality implies that the b value in $y = mx + b$ must be zero. At this point, I assign Exercise 31.

With the following four examples, I talk about proportions being linear, quadratic, joint or inverse. Also, I mention the constant of proportionality and what information is necessary to determine the constant of proportionality. This is also a good time to discuss unit analysis and how most of the constants, k, have units attached to them so that each side of the equation has the same units!

1. $F = kx$, spring force

2. $A = kr^2$, area of a circle of radius r

3. $V = kr^2h$, volume of a cylinder

4. $r = \dfrac{k}{t}$, from $d = rt$, the idea here is that for a given distance (the constant of proportionality) time and rate are inversely proportional.

At this point, I have the students work on Exercises 37, 39, and 53.

Wrap-up. I conclude this section by pointing out how many real-life applications there are for proportionality. If there is time I talk about what happens to a circumference and area of a circle, and volume of a sphere when the radius is doubled or tripled. This gets at the idea that proportionality is not always linear!

Coaching for Homework

(5 minutes): *Exercises 39 to 40, 50 to 57 use quadratic variation and joint variation.*

Section 5.2 Inverse Variation and Related Graphs

Preparation   **Objectives**
- Identify variation as direct or inverse.
- Find the constant of variation.
- Use inverse variation formulas in applications.
- Graph inverse variation equations.
- Identify the behavior of a graph near an input that gives an undefined output.
- Find the axis of symmetry in inverse variation graphs.

Links
- Graphing: Sections 1.2, 5.5, and 5.6.
- Scientific notation: Section 6.0.
- Hyperbola: Section 8.4
- *Mirror, Mirror* activity in IRM Section 2.1.

Time and Emphasis
50 minutes. Optional material.

Points to Stress
- Identify how to find inverse variation (products are the same) and direct variation (ratios are the same).
- Determine how to find the constant of proportionality; this includes emphasizing the units in an equation.

> **NOTE**
> The second part of this section includes a discussion of rational functions. This should be kept at a very introductory level.
> Introducing the idea of an asymptote is easily done if you include a practical example in the discussion.

Suggested Lesson Format
Warm-up: 10 minutes

Lecture/Group Activity: 35 minutes

Coaching for Homework: 5 minutes

Materials Needed for Class
Graph paper

Graphing calculator

Borrow a turntable from the Physics Lab (optional)

Homework Assignment
Core Exercises: 1 to 19, odd. (This does not include any work on rational functions).

Sample assignment: 1 to 33, odd.

> **For Labs and Recitations**
> Return to *Mirror, Mirror* (Section 2.1, IRM page 36). Identify the information given and results found in terms of direct or inverse variation. Is the relationship between the number of images and angle between the mirrors a direct or an inverse variation? What is the constant of variation?

In Class

Warm-up

(5 minutes): Have the students work in groups filling out an input-output table and plotting points for $y = \dfrac{1}{x}$. Ask what happens to y as x gets greater. What happens to y as x gets close to zero? Be sure to plot values of $|x| < 1$. Ask the students to describe (in sentence form) the difference in this graph from the linear or quadratic graphs that they have already seen.

Lecture/Group Activity

Graph $y = \dfrac{1}{x}$. on an overhead calculator and ask whether the graph "disappears." Is it connected at $x = 0$? This is a good time to teach students about the connect and disconnect mode on the calculator. It is helpful for students to realize that their calculators' graphs are discrete rather than continuous. Also, changing the viewing window helps convince students that there really are values besides integers.

If you can borrow a turntable from your physics classroom to bring in for a demonstration about angular velocity you can demonstrate an inverse variation; $w = \dfrac{k}{r}$ where w is the angular velocity and r is the radius. A turntable that students can stand on is a great way to show students why ice skaters bring their arms in to speed up and spread them out to slow down.

> **Avoiding the Pitfalls** Many students do not understand that if the left-hand side of an equation represents something like the number of apples in a barrel, then the right-hand side of the equation must also represent the number of apples in a barrel. The constant of proportionality is the key to making sure that the units match on both sides of the equation. Sometimes students think that because the constant of proportionality is a constant that it does not have units (like Pi). Be sure to include units in all of your examples.

The next inverse variation that students can relate to is Example 2. Use your current state lottery value (if you have one). Also talk about scaling the graph so that you can get all of the data on the plot. Another good example is Exercise 2.

> **NOTE**
> None of the direct variations in Example 8 and Exercises 7 to 16 happened to have negative slopes so students might need a the following example to show a decreasing function that is not an inverse variation:
>
> On a recent dive, a research submarine recorded its time and position relative to sea level as (2 minutes, –400 feet) and (5 minutes, –1000 feet). Is the submarine position a direct variation?

Looking at Exercises 11 and 12 in the is a good way to demonstrate the differences between direct and indirect variation.

Do Exercise 26 in class to sum up rational functions. Have the students work on Exercises 32 and 34 in groups.

Wrap-up. Sum up by talking about teeter-totters. Ask students if the relationship between placement from the fulcrum and weight of the child is direct or indirect.

Coaching for Homework

(5 minutes): Remind students to use units with all of the applied problems.

When graphing multiple graphs on one set of axes, set the scale so a comparison can be made. If the scale is too large the graphs are indistinguishable.

Exercise 40 uses scientific notation (see Section 6.0 as needed).

Section 5.3 Simplification, Multiplication, and Division of Rational Expressions

Preparation

Objectives
- Find when a rational expression is not defined.
- Simplify rational expressions.
- Multiply and divide rational expressions.
- Simplify complex fractions.
- Multiply and divide expressions containing units of measure.

Links
- Factoring: Sections 3.0, and 4.0.
- Units of measure: Sections 5.0, and 5.1.
- Rational numbers: Section 5.0.
- Complex fractions: Section 5.4.
- Solving equations: Section 5.6.

Time and Emphasis
50 minutes. Essential material.

Vocabulary

additive inverse   complex fractions   rational expressions   reciprocal

Points to Stress
- When the numerator and denominator of a fraction are the same, the fraction equals 1.
- When the numerator and denominator of a fraction are additive inverses, the fraction equals −1.
- To multiply rational expressions, write the product with a single numerator and denominator. Factor as needed. Eliminate common factors from the numerator and denominator. Multiply remaining factors in the numerator and in the denominator.

> **NOTE** Including units, such as miles per hour divided by gallons per hour, helps students visualize the simplification of complex expressions.

> Avoiding the Pitfalls
> For rational expressions there are several pitfalls that students can hit. This section looks at several of these and tries to encourage students to keep in mind the difference between factors and terms.

- To divide rational expressions, multiply the first expression by the reciprocal of the second expression.
- Simplify complex fractions by first writing the fraction as a division.

Suggested Lesson Format
Warm-up: 5 minutes
Lecture/Group Activity: 40 minutes
Coaching on Homework: 5 minutes

Materials Needed for Class
Copies of *Not-So-Simple Fractions* (IRM page 95).

Homework Assignment
Core exercises: 11 to 31, odd; 35 to 47, odd
Sample assignment: 1 to 49, odd.

For Labs and Recitations

Comparing ages by ratios, Example 1, is an activity that can be done with many levels of classes from arithmetic through calculus. Students make a table using the headings shown in Table 9 and then complete it for a mother-child pair with whom they are familiar. One key idea is to distinguish the types of functions created by each column in the table when the child's age is the input. The mother's age is a linear function. The difference in ages is a constant function. The ratio of ages, mother to child, is a rational function with an undefined value when the child is born (due to the division by zero).

The associated Think about it 1 suggests exploring when the ratio of ages will be 2 to 1 and whether the ratio can ever be 1 to 1. The setting extends to limits in calculus. Additional questions, using the graphing calculator, are found in the project in Exercise 54.

In Class

Warm-up

(5 minutes): Do the warm-up at the beginning of the section. Encourage students to practice factoring if this is not a strength for them. This section gives lots of opportunity to practice. The idea is for students to become proficient at factoring so that difficulty working with rational expressions is not compounded by lack of factoring ability.

Lecture/Group Activity

(40 minutes): Undefined values. For the undefined values, put several expressions on the board and talk about what values would make the denominator zero. Also, ask students why this is of concern (remind them of the asymptotes from the previous section).

Additive inverses. For understanding additive inverses of expressions, set up an input-output table for an expression such as $y = (x - 1)/(1 - x)$. After the students are convinced what the y values are, have them graph this in the standard window. Ask why there is a hole at $x = 1$.

Simplifying rational expressions. Practice simplifying rational expressions, emphasizing that terms can not be canceled, but factors can be. Ask students why this is so.

Multiplying and dividing rational expressions. Practice multiplying and dividing rational expressions and assign some practice from Exercises 41 to 50.

Assign *Not-So-Simple Fractions* to be done in groups.

Wrap-up. Remind students that rational expressions are challenging due to the number of algorithmic steps needed to simplify these expressions. Encourage students to make 3-by-5 note cards to study with examples of each operation.

NOTE Exercises 49 to 52 show common errors in simplifying rational expressions. These might be done as a group warm-up on the following day.

Coaching for Homework

(5 minutes): *In Exercises 13 to 20, 23 to 32, and 35 to 38, be sure to factor before doing any simplification*

As you do Exercises 39 to 48, think of settings or applications where these units might appear.

Not-So-Simple Fractions

1. Find the value(s) of x for which the following expressions are undefined:

a. $\dfrac{2x-1}{3-x}$

b. $\dfrac{2x-1}{3x}$

c. $\dfrac{2x-1}{x^2-7x+10}$

2.   Simplify the expressions:

a. $\dfrac{4x}{6y}$

b. $\dfrac{3x(x+2)}{6xy}$

c. $\dfrac{xy+y^2}{xy}$

3. The additive inverse of an expression is achieved by taking the opposite sign of the expression. For example, the additive inverse of 2 is -2. The additive inverse of $-x$ is x. The additive inverse of $1 - x$ is $-1 + x$. Find the additive inverses of the following expressions.

a. $1 + a$

b. $3 - 5x$

c. $x - 7y$

Section 5.4 Addition and Subtraction of Rational Expressions

Preparation

Objectives
- Find the common denominator for two or more rational expressions.
- Add and subtract rational expressions with like denominators.
- Add and subtract rational expressions with unlike denominators.
- Simplify complex fractions.

Links
- Rational numbers: Section 5.0.
- Complex fractions: Section 5.3.
- Least common denominator: Section 5.6

Time and Emphasis
50 minutes. Essential material.

Vocabulary
complex rational expressions

Points to Stress
- To find the least common denominator, form a product by including each factor the highest number of times it appears in any denominator.
- To add or subtract rational numbers, convert to a common denominator, if needed; add or subtract the numerators and place the result over the common denominator; factor and simplify the answer.
- Simplify complex fractions by multiplying the numerator and denominator by the least common denominator of all terms.

Suggested Lesson Format
Warm-up: 5 minutes

Questions on Homework: 10 minutes

Lecture/Group Activity: 25 minutes

Coaching for Homework: 5 minutes

Materials Needed for Class
None

Homework
Core Exercises: 1 to 21, odd.

Sample Assignment: 1 to 31, odd; 39 to 45, odd.

Optional Activity
Simplifying Complex Fractions (IRM pages 98 and 99).

For Labs and Recitations
Students working in pairs should do Exercises 47 to 50 and write out clues that suggest how to predict the missing operations.

In Class

Warm-up

(5 minutes): Assign the Warm-up to be done individually. Warm-up Exercises 1 to 6 review computation with fractions. Warm-ups 7 to 9 provide exploration with multiplication by least common denominators in simplifying complex rational expressions.

Questions on Homework

(10 minutes): Have the students go over the homework in groups and select questions for class discussion.

Lecture/Group Activity

(25 minutes): Adding and subtracting rational expressions. The average-trip-speed setting in Examples 1 and 2 provides results that both surprise students and utilize rational expressions. Have students explore Example 1 in pairs. Generalize the setting to two equal distances, x, in discussing Example 2 with the whole class. Adding fractions and recognizing the need for a common denominator are essential skills in both Examples.

Discuss the role of factoring and finding least common denominator in adding rational expressions, then have the students work in pairs to add or subtract the expressions given in Examples 4, 5, 6, and 7.

Complex rational expressions. Return to the average trip speed and apply the least common denominator for the variable expressions found in Example 10.

Return to the Warm-up Exercises 7 to 9 to introduce a second method for simplifying complex fractions. Have students work Example 11 in pairs.

Coaching for Homework

(5 minutes): *When there is a possibility of a zero-valued denominator, make not of the restrictions on the variables.*

When you set up common denominators and when you simplify answers, be sure to show all factoring clearly.

Refer to Examples 1, 2 or 9 in solving Exercises 25 to 32.

Simplifying Complex Fractions

Start here:

The following set of expressions form a closed system under the operation of substitution (known in higher courses as composition of functions).

$$A: \frac{1}{1-x}; \quad B: \frac{x-1}{x}$$

$$C: \frac{x}{x-1}; \quad D: \frac{1}{x}$$

$$E: 1-x; \quad F: x$$

Example substitutions:

A into A gives $\dfrac{1}{1-\left(\dfrac{1}{1-x}\right)}$ and simplifies to $\dfrac{x-1}{x}$ or B.

Do the simplification by hand to check the result.

A into B gives $\dfrac{\left(\dfrac{1}{1-x}\right)-1}{\left(\dfrac{1}{1-x}\right)}$ and simplifies to x, or F.

Do the simplification by hand to check the result.

The results for A into A and A into B are shown in the table below.

	A	B	F
A	B	F	
B			
F			

Within your group, complete the table for the expressions A, B, and F.

Extensions:

1. Identities.

   When we multiply 1 times an expression, *n*, the answer is *n*. We say 1 is the multiplicative identity.
   When we add 0 to an expression, *n*, the answer is *n*. We say 0 is the *additive identity*.
   When we substitute _____ in each expression, *n*, the answer is *n*. We say expression _____ is the *substitution identity*.

2. Inverses.

   When we multiply a number by its reciprocal (or *multiplicative inverse*), we get 1, the multiplicative identity.
   When we add a number to its opposite (or *additive inverse*), we get 0, the additive identity.
   When we substitute ___ into ___ and ____ into ____ we get *x*, the substitution identity.
   The two expressions, ___ and ___, are called inverses.

3. An extended project.

   To complete the full table for all six expressions, there are 36 different substitutions to perform: each of *A*, *B*, *C*, *D*, *E*, and *F* (on the left side of the table) is substituted into each expression (listed across the top of the table).

	A	*B*	*C*	*D*	*E*	*F*
A	*B*	*F*				
B						
C						
D						
E						
F						

4. Does *F* continue to be the identity in the full table?

5. *A* into *B* and *B* into *A* gave the identity *x* (expression *F*). *A* and *B* are inverses. Is there another pair of expressions like *A* and *B* that when substituted into each other give *x*, the identity.

6. Which expressions give *x* when substituted into themselves?

Section 5.5 Division of Polynomials and Related Graphs

Preparation

Objectives
- Graph selected rational expressions.
- Divide polynomial expressions using long division.
- Find whether a divisor is a factor of the dividend.
- Use long division to factor cubic expressions.

Links
- Factoring sums and differences of cubes: Section 4.0.
- Graphs of polynomial and rational functions: Sections 4.0, 5.2, and 5.6.

Time and Emphasis

50 minutes. Optional material.

Vocabulary

asymptote

Points to Stress
- Division of polynomials is similar to long division of numbers.
- Division gives a way to factor sums and differences of cubes if we forget the second factor.
- To divide algebraic expressions we arrange the dividend into descending order of exponents and replace missing terms with terms having a zero numerical coefficient.
- When there is no remainder in a polynomial division, we say the divisor is a factor of the dividend.
- A zero remainder indicates that the graph of the expression will contain a hole with an x-coordinate that makes a zero denominator in the original rational expression.
- A non-zero remainder indicates that the graph will have a nearly vertical portion near the x-coordinate that makes a zero denominator in the original rational expression.

Suggested Lesson Format

Warm-up: 5 minutes
Questions on Homework: 10 minutes
Lecture/Group Activity: 25 minutes
Coaching for Homework: 5 minutes

Materials Needed for Class

None

Homework

<u>Core Exercises</u>: 1 to 11, odd; 19 to 25, odd; 29 to 33, odd.
<u>Sample Assignment</u>: 1 to 37, odd; 43, and 45.

Optional Activity

Practice factoring cubes with the project in Exercise 53.

For Labs and Recitations

Do additional long division practice, such as with Exercises 30 to 36, even.

Investigate the relationship between the value of a function, f(a), and division by x - a, in Exercises 47 and 48.

In Class   **Warm-up**

(5 minutes): Assign the Warm-up to be done individually.

Questions on Homework

(10 minutes): Have the students go over the homework in groups and select questions for class discussion.

Lecture/Group Activity

Introduction. Explain to the class that Warm-up Exercises 1 and 2 practice long division. Warm up Exercise 1 is used in parallel with the polynomial division to show steps. Exercises 3 to 6 practice subtraction steps found within the polynomial division.

Example 1 shows that we should expect that the division of a cubic polynomial by a linear polynomial results in a quadratic polynomial (shown by the parabolic shape of the graph).

Polynomial division. From Example 1, we predict that the answer to the division in Example 2 should start with an x^2 term. Introduce the vocabulary of division and then the parallel arithmetic and polynomial divisions in Example 2.

Have the students work in pairs on using long division to divide the expression in Example 3. Examine the graph in Example 3. It again permits us to predict a quadratic result. The question arises as to how to get like terms within the division process and motivates placing terms with zero coefficients into the dividend.

Have pairs of students divide another problem that comes out even, such as Exercise 30, $(x^4 - 1)/(x - 1)$, and then one that does not come out even, such as Example 6. Figures 27, 28, and 29 show the effect of the non-zero remainder on the parabolic graph found earlier.

Stress that the graphs of the division problems have either a hole or nearly vertical parts as a result of places where the original expression is undefined but do not expect students to graph these by hand.

Coaching for Homework

(5 minutes): *Observe that sets of exercises (1 to 11, odd; 2 to 12, even; 19 to 25, odd; 20 to 26, even) have the same numerators but different denominators. Look for patterns in the results from divisions.*

Exercises 13 to 18 suggest ways of looking for patterns.

Section 5.6 Solving Rational Equations

Preparation

Objectives

- Find the least common denominator of rational expressions in an equation.
- Solve equations containing rational expressions.
- Solve equations graphically.
- Solve application problems related to $\dfrac{1}{a} + \dfrac{1}{b} = \dfrac{1}{c}$
- Solve application problems containing rational expressions.

Links

- Proportions: Section 5.1.
- Graphs of polynomial and rational functions: Sections 4.0, 5.2, and 5.5.
- Least common denominator: Section 5.4.
- Systems of equations: Section 8.0.

Time and Emphasis

50 minutes. Essential material.

Vocabulary

extraneous root   rational equations   system of equations

Points to Stress

- When a rational equation is in the form of a proportion, $\dfrac{a}{b} = \dfrac{c}{d}$, the equation may be cross multiplied to a $\bullet$ d = b $\bullet$ c and then solved.
- To eliminate denominators in an equation, multiply each side by the least common denominator.
- A summary table for linear, quadratic, and rational equations is shown on page 400.

Suggested Lesson Format

Warm-up: 5 minutes
Questions on Homework: 10 minutes
Lecture/Group Activity: 25 minutes
Coaching for Homework: 5 minutes

Materials Needed for Class

None

Homework

Core Exercises: 1 to 7, odd; 17 to 23, odd; 33 to 59, every other odd.
Sample Assignment: 1 to 71, every other odd. Choose more as needed.

For Labs and Recitations

Have the students work in pairs on the project in Exercise 89, Proportion Proofs.

In Class   **Warm-up**

(5 minutes): As a Warm-up, have the students solve the equations stated in Examples 1 and 2 to review solving equations and formulas.

Questions on Homework

(10 minutes): Have the students go over the homework in groups and select questions for class discussion.

Lecture/Group Activity

Solving proportions by cross multiplication. Have students solve the equation in Example 3 with cross multiplication and then set up the graphing calculator solution to verify their work.

Reverse the procedure in Example 4. Use the graph to predict the number of solutions and then find the solutions by hand, with cross multiplication. Introduce extraneous roots by showing that one of the solutions by hand in Example 4 does not satisfy the equation, nor does it show on the graph as a solution.

Solving equations with the least common denominator.

Examples 5 and 6 solve the same equation with different methods. The first example solves by changing the equation to a proportion and then cross multiplying. The second multiplies both sides by the least common denominator. Have students solve the equation in Example 6 individually and then compare their steps in pairs. They can read Example 5 on their own later to see how the equation might have been solved with a proportion.

Have the students solve Example 7 individually and again compare their steps in pairs.

Applications. Return to theater exits in Example 8 and develop an equation of the form $\frac{1}{a}+\frac{1}{b}=\frac{1}{c}$. Note to students that the equation is solved in Example 9. Discuss the many applications of this equation, as listed on page 393.

Coaching for Homework

(5 minutes): *Check solutions to equations to verify that no answer gives a zero denominator.*

Exercises 65 to 72 require formulas listed on page 393.

The applications of ratios and proportions in Exercises 73 to 76 are modeled after Example 10.

Exercises 77 to 82 provide practice in solving formulas containing denominators.

Section 6.0 Review of Exponents and Scientific Notation

Preparation

Objectives
- Simplify expressions containing zero and negative numbers as exponents.
- Find products, quotients, and powers of exponential expressions.
- Change numbers between decimal notation and scientific notation.
- Use a calculator to do operations with scientific notation, and write answers with appropriate significant digits.

Links
- Exponents: Section 1.0, 6.1, and 6.2.
- Properties of powers: Section 6.2 .

Time and Emphasis
10 minutes. Essential review material.

Vocabulary

digits	–1 exponents	–2 exponents
placeholders	power	power properties
product property of like bases	quotient property of like bases	scientific notation
significant digits	zero exponents	

Points to Stress
- The definition of exponents is expanded to include any integer as an exponent with $b^0 = 1$ and $b^{-n} = \dfrac{1}{b^n}$ for $\neq 0$

- The product, quotient, and power properties of exponents apply to any integer as an exponent.
- Numbers in scientific notation have one nonzero digit before the decimal point.
- Significant digits include zeros between nonzero digits, zeros following a nonzero digit after a decimal point, and zeros that are placeholders and are marked with an overbar.

Suggested Lesson Format
Post-test reading and exercise assignment.
Lecture/Group Activity: 5 minutes (on significant digits) with Section 6.1
Coaching for Homework: 5 minutes (on day prior to the test)

Materials Needed for Class
None

Homework
Core exercises: 1 to 9, odd; 23 to 33, odd.

Sample assignment: 1 to 13, odd; 17, 23 to 33, odd; 37.

Optional Activities
Review skills from rational expressions, Chapter 5, with Exercises 19 to 22.
Connect exponents and probability with the project in Exercise 41.

For Labs and Recitations
Discuss the display of scientific notation on non-graphing calculators, Exercise 35.
Review unit analysis with scientific notation, Exercise 38. Other scientific notation problems were included in projects in Chapter 5: Section 5.1, Exercise 65 and Section 5.2, Exercise 40.

In Class

Warm-up

(5 minutes): Assign the Warm-up to be done individually.

Lecture/Group Activity

(5 minutes): Assign reading and exercises for this section as a follow-up to a test covering through Chapter 5. Mention that you will review the concept of significant digits, if needed, before continuing on to Section 6.1.

. Mention that the Warm-up reviews powers of 2, 3, 4, 5, and 10. Knowing these helps understand and remember the concepts in this and the next chapter.

Prompt the students to use the expressions and answers in Example 1 to write rules for zero and negative integer exponents before reading on.

Coaching for Homework

See, also, Optional Activity above.

TIP Under [MODE] on graphing calculators, there is a third option in addition to normal and scientific notation: ENG, which represents engineering notation.

Engineering notation is a form of scientific notation in which the exponent on 10 is limited to a multiple of 3. The number 13,000 is written 13×10^3 in engineering notation. Engineering notation facilitates work with units because such metric prefixes as kilo-, mega-, and giga- represent 10^3, 10^6, and 10^9, respectively. Think carefully about this when marking student answers in scientific notation. How important is it whether the student writes 13×10^3 (engineering notation) or 1.3×10^4?

NOTE Throughout this chapter emphasize that the answer to the expression 2^5 is the power. We say the 5th power of 2 is 8. The number 5 is the exponent.

Functions of the form, $f(x) = ax^n$, are called power functions because they contain the nth power of a variable. We return to power functions and their solution, with roots, in Section 6.4. We solve exponential functions $y = ab^x$ with logarithms in Section 7.3.

Section 6.1 Rational Exponents

Preparation

Objectives
- Use a calculator to explore powers with integer bases.
- Evaluate exponential expressions with and without a calculator.
- Apply rational exponents in settings involving compound interest and body fat composition.

Links
- Exponents and Powers: Section 6.0.
- Compound interest: Sections 6.4, 7.3, and 7.5.

Time and Emphasis
50 minutes. Essential material.

Vocabulary

exponential equation   rational exponent   recursive formula

Points to Stress
- Knowing powers of 2, 3, 4, 5, and 10 facilitates learning these concepts.
- If $b^{1/n}$ is defined, $b^{m/n} = (b^m)^{1/n} = (b^{1/n})^m$.
- Rational exponents may appear both in power equations, $y = x^n$, and in exponential equations, $y = b^x$.
- The compound interest formula, $A = P(1 + r/n)^{nt}$, simplifies to annual interest, $A = P(1 + r)^t$ when interest is compounded once a year.

Suggested Lesson Format
Warm-up: 5 minutes
Questions on Homework: 10 minutes
Lecture/Group Activity: 25 minutes
Coaching for Homework: 5 minutes

Materials Needed For Class
None

Homework
Core exercises: 7 to 11, odd; 19, 21, 25, 27, 39 to 45, odd.
Sample assignment: 1 to 33, odd; 37 to 45, odd.

Optional Activity
The Body Composition formulas, Example 12, use decimal exponents.
Exercises 49 to 54 practice these formulas.

For Labs and Recitations
Practice mentally calculating exponential expressions with the project in Exercise 55. Investigate what the worth is today of the $24 in trade goods that is said to have been paid by the Dutch director-general Peter Minuit in 1626 to the Native Americans for Manhattan Island. Assume 7% interest compounded annually.

In Class

Warm-up

(5 minutes):Assign the Warm-up to be done individually.

Questions on Homework

(10 minutes):Have the students go over the homework in groups and select questions for class discussion.

Lecture/Group Activity

(25 minutes): Rational Exponents. Start by having the students solve the equations in Example 1 by guess and check on the calculator. Remind students to write their answers in both fraction and decimal notation.

Have the students use the graph of $y = 4^x$ in Example 2 to check Parts b, f, and i in Example 1.

Define rational exponent.

It is possible to group the factors of a number to show the rational exponent, Example 3. Read through Example 3 with the class and have students, in pairs, discuss the placement of the parentheses in Parts a, b, c, and d. At the top of page 421, $8^{1/3} = 2$ because 2 is one of three equal factors; $81^{1/4} = 3$ because 3 is one of four equal factors. Have students work Examples 4 and 5 in pairs.

Compound interest. Example 6 suggests how the annual compound interest formula ($n = 1$) is derived and Example 7 suggests how the full compound interest formula ($n \neq 1$) is derived. Discuss those examples if the derivation is important.

Draw a figure like that shown below to help students visualize how the number of compoundings in one year is related to the interest applied at each compounding.

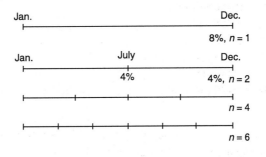

Have the students complete the figure by labeling the months and interest rates paid for a January 1 deposit compounded quarterly, and every two months. Assume the annual rate remains 8%. [Answer: For $n = 4$, 2% every three months; and for $n = 6$, 1 1/3% every two months.]

Have the students work in pairs to evaluate the compound interest formula for the settings in Example 9 and 10. Example 9 shows how a small amount of money invested for a long period of time grows to a sizable amount. Example 10 contains rational exponents, remind students to change the mixed numbers into decimals when they substitute into the formula.

FUN ALERT

It is said that Benjamin Franklin did not believe that public officials should be paid and donated his salary to the state of Pennsylvania on the condition that it not be spent for 100 years.

At the end of that time, a dispute over how to spend the money arose and the expenditure was delayed another 100 years. Example 9 shows the growth of $1 in a 200 year investment and consequently why there may have been disagreement over the expenditure.

Have students identify the coefficient, base, and exponent in the equation in Example 11.

Coaching for Homework

(5 minutes): Exercises 29 and 30 will help you understand the meaning of the parts of the compound interest formula in a word problem setting.

Section 6.2 Roots and Rational Exponents

Preparation

Objectives
- Simplify nth root expressions.
- Change expressions from rational exponent to radical notation and vice versa.
- Use properties of powers and radicals to simplify expressions.

Links
- Product property of square roots: Section 3.1.
- Quotient property of square roots: Section 3.3.
- Principal square roots: Sections 3.1, and 3.3.
- Absolute value: Sections 1.0, 2.4, and 3.3.
- Complex numbers: Section 4.3.
- Exponents: Sections 1.0, 6.0.

Time and Emphasis
50 minutes. Essential material.

Vocabulary

cube root	index of a radical	nth root	power properties
principal nth root	principal square root	radical sign	

Points to Stress

- For all numbers b for which $\sqrt[n]{b}$ is defined, $\sqrt[n]{b} = b^{\frac{1}{n}}$.
- No real number can be raised to any even power to obtain a negative number.
- A negative real number raised to any odd power yields a negative number.
- If n is odd, $b^{n/n} = b$. If n is even, $b^{n/n} = |b|$.
- If $\dfrac{m}{n}$ is a rational number in lowest terms, and if $\sqrt[n]{b}$ is defined, then

$$b^{\frac{m}{n}} = (b^{\frac{1}{n}})^m = \left(\sqrt[n]{b}\right)^m = \sqrt[n]{b^m}$$

- The power properties of rational exponents can be extended to radical expressions for base b, b > 0.

Suggested Lesson Format

Warm-up: 5 minutes

Lecture/Group Activity: 25 minutes

Coaching for Homework: 5 minutes

Optional Activities

The project in Exercise 53 suggests a more general distributive property. We might describe the general distributive property as being able to distribute operations listed in any column of the table at right over operations in the columns immediately to the left. We may not skip over a column or distribute within the same column or distribut[e]

Materials Needed for Class

Calculators with rational exponent key

Homework

Core exercises: 19 to 43, every third problem. (This gives the most practice in simplifying expressions.)

Sample assignment: 1 to 51, odd.

Avoiding the Pitfalls

Use the figure below to help visual learners remember the general distributive property.

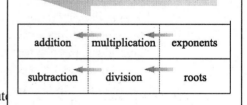

Distribute one column to the left.

addition	multiplication	exponents
subtraction	division	roots

For Labs and Recitations
Examples 45 and 46 combine work with radical expressions, units, and scientific notation. Do these in groups of three and ask for a record sheet showing all steps.

In Class

Warm-up

(10 minutes): Assign the Warm-up to be done in groups. Have the students compare answers. For Exercise 3, remind the students to use of the absolute value sign when taking a squared term from under the radical sign. After the students have completed the Warm-up, go over Exercise 3 so that all students recall the use of the absolute value when using radicals. This helps when taking, for example, the fourth root of the fourth power of a variable.

Lecture/Group Activity

(35 minutes): Begin by tying together the Warm-up with Exercises like 16 and 18. Ask students how the square root sign and the exponent $\frac{1}{2}$ are related. Then ask about the cube root sign and how they would write this as an exponent. Some students already have seen this notation, but others will have more "buy in" if given the opportunity to come up with the idea of the nth root being the exponent $\frac{1}{n}$. Point out the key stroke on their calculators. This can take considerable time if more than one or two calculators are present in the room. A short cut may be to use the $\wedge$ key, reminding students to use parentheses for $\frac{1}{n}$.

Move from here to the nth root of the mth power of an expression in radical form. Students get more understanding from seeing lots of examples than from explanations, so at this point doing several examples is a good idea.

Try Exercises 22 and 26. Go back to the idea of the absolute value and principal roots. Also, give a quick review of the properties of exponents. Remind the students that although they have just learned about rational exponents, these exponents follow the same rules as integer exponents with the exception of the absolute value and watching for negative bases with even roots. Do Exercise 32 with the class to back this up.

Refer the students to the steps in the box on page 435 for simplifying radical expressions. This may be helpful when the students are practicing the problems. Activity. Have the students work in groups on Exercises 42 and 44. Since each of these problems has several parts, have individual groups put one problem (include all steps) on the board.

Wrap-up. The wrap-up becomes checking the work that the groups have put up on the board. Going over the steps (process) and pointing out areas that may be challenging is very helpful.

Coaching for Homework

(5 minutes): *Exercises 1 to 10 illustrate the product and quotient properties for square roots, first numerically and then with symbols.*

In Exercises 19 to 22, write each expression with a rational exponent as a root expression and visa versa.

The numerical exercises, 11 to 18, 23 to 26, 31 to 34 are to be done mentally.

The restriction, if $\sqrt[n]{x}$ is defined, in the boxes on page 432 is subtle. The expression $\sqrt[6]{x^2}$ is defined for all x, but $\left(\sqrt[6]{x}\right)^2$ requires that $x \geq 0$. Thus, in Exercises 25, 26, and 30, the $\left(\sqrt[n]{x}\right)^m = x^{\frac{m}{n}}$ only if $\sqrt[n]{x}$ is defined.

Warn the students that Exercises 47 to 51 may require some thought and time to do.

Section 6.3 More Operations with Radicals

Preparation

Objectives
- Add and subtract radicals.
- Multiply two- and three-term radical expressions.
- Identify the conjugate of a radical expression.
- Rationalize the numerator or denominator of a radical expression.

Links
- Quadratic formula: Section 3.4.
- Radical expressions: Section 6.2.

Time and Emphasis
50 minutes. Essential material.

Vocabulary

conjugate products	distance formula (in exercises)	rationalizing
real-number conjugates	similar radicals	

Points to Stress
- Radical expressions can be added or subtracted if they can be changed to similar radicals.
- To multiply multiple-term radical expressions, apply the distributive property.
- The product of real number conjugates is a rational number.
- To rationalize a one-term expression, multiply by a number whose product with the radical makes an exact root.
- To rationalize a two-term expression, multiply by the conjugate.
- The distance formula and Hero's formula (for area) are applications of radicals included in the exercises.

Suggested Lesson Format
Warm-up: 5 minutes
Questions on Homework: 10 minutes
Lecture/Group Activity: 25 minutes
Coaching for Homework: 5 minutes

NOTE Stress simplification of radical expressions containing numbers only to permit students to think more clearly about radical expressions containing variables.

Materials Needed for Class
None

Homework
Core Exercises: 1 to 31, odd; 39 to 49, odd; 55, 57, and 59.
Sample assignment: 1 to 49, odd; 55, 57, 59, and 61.

For Labs and Recitations
Derive the distance formula, Exercise 55.
Do the project, Minimum Cost, in Exercise 65.

In Class   **Warm-up**

(5 minutes): Assign the Warm-up to be done individually.

Questions on Homework

(10 minutes):Have the students go over the homework in groups and select questions for class discussion.

Lecture/Group Activity

(25 minutes): Motivation for addition and subtraction of radicals. Start with the text Warm-up on solving quadratic equations with the quadratic formula: *Recall that we check solutions to an equation by substituting the numbers for x. In the Warm-up we found radical expressions as solutions. When we substitute these numbers into the original equations and simplify, we must multiply and add with radicals.*

Have the students substitute solutions into the equations from the Warm-up and discover in what steps they need help.

Define similar radicals and addition (and subtraction) of radicals. Have the students work in pairs on Example 3.

Multiplication of two or more terms containing radicals. Encourage the students to use a table for organizing multiplication of multiple terms. Have students work in pairs to do Example 5.

Conjugates and rationalizing. Define conjugates and their role in rationalizing two-term expressions.

Have students do Example 6, 7 and 8. Note, if time, that Example 10 contains a proof where rationalization is needed in a step. See also the project in Exercise 77, page 281.

Coaching for Homework

(5 minutes): *Note that the exercises move progressively from numerical to symbolic, 1 to 24, and again in 25 to 32.*

The golden ratio mentioned in Exercise 37 was first seen in the golden rectangle discussion in Section 3.4.

Exercise 55 introduces the distance formula. If you are not already familiar with it, learn it by writing it in full for each of Exercises 56 to 61.

NOTE The product $\left(\sqrt{a}-\sqrt{b}\right)\left(\sqrt{a}+\sqrt{b}\right)$ gives a different answer from $\left(-\sqrt{a}+\sqrt{b}\right)\left(\sqrt{a}+\sqrt{b}\right)$ Rather than worrying about which is the correct conjugate, note that either can be used to obtain equivalent rationalized expression for $\dfrac{1}{\left(\sqrt{a}+\sqrt{b}\right)}$.

Section 6.4 Inverse Functions: Solving Power and Root Equations

Preparation

Objectives
- Find the inverse of a function from a table, from a graph, and from an equation.
- Identify power and root functions.
- Solve a power equation by taking the nth root of both sides.
- Solve a radical equation by taking the nth power of both sides.

Links
- Inverse equations (exponential and logarithmic equations): Section 7.2.
- Compound interest: Sections 6.1, 7.3, and 7.5.

Time and Emphasis

Two 50-minute sessions. Essential material.

Vocabulary

depreciation   extraneous roots   inflation   inverse function

power function   root function

Points to Stress

> **NOTE** In this text, we do not rationalize formula expressions. Hence in Example 10 we leave the formula with a radical applying to a denominator.

- Inverse functions can be found in three ways: with tables, graphs, or algebra.
- To find the inverse from the table for a function, swap the input and output (x and y) columns and find the rule for the new table. Check whether the inverse is a function.
- To find the inverse from the graph of a function, swap the numbers (x, y) in each ordered pair and plot the resulting graph. Check whether the inverse is a function.
- To find the inverse from the equation of a function, swap x and y in the equation and in the restrictions and solve (if possible) for y.
- Inverse operations and functions permit us to solve equations. With some restrictions, nth power functions and nth root (or radical) functions are inverses and may be used to solve the other form of the equation.
- Solving power and root equations can introduce false solutions so students need to check their answers to these equations. In addition to false solutions, no solutions can also occur.
- To use the compound interest formula for annual rate of growth, inflation, or depreciation, let $n = 1$ in $A = P(1 + r/n)^{nt}$.

Suggested Lesson Format

Warm-up: 10 minutes

Lecture/Group Activity: 35 minutes (first day)

Coaching for Homework: 5 minutes (first day)

Lecture: 25 minutes (second day)

Practice Activity: 15 minutes (second day)

> **NOTE** In Section 6.1 we evaluated compound interest formulas, here we solve for rates by using inverse power and radical functions, and in Sections 7.3 and 7.5 we will solve for time using another pair of inverses: exponential and logarithmic functions.

Materials Needed for Class

Graphing calculator

Graph paper

Homework

Core exercises: 9 to 19, odd; 59 to 75, odd.

Sample assignment: 1 to 25, odd (first day covers inverse functions). 27 to 83, every third problem (second day covers practice problems and applications).

For Labs and Recitations

Do the projects in Exercises 90, 91, and 92 to look at applications for power regression. In Exercise 90, Part c, the exact area under a square root curve and between the origin and a vertical line at x is $A = (2/3)x^{3/2}$

In Class   **Warm-up**

(10 minutes): Assign the Warm-up to be done individually. The Warm-up exercises illustrate how the inverse operations undo the original operation and are a good way to introduce inverse functions. It is a good idea to give some motivation as to why we might need inverse functions. The idea of knowing y and determining x is an excellent way to motivate this subject especially if put into an applied context.

Lecture/Group Activity (first day)

(40 minutes): Inverse functions. Introduce the concept of finding an inverse function using graphs and tables with Example 1. Ask the students to determine the rule for the inverse function.

Avoiding the Pitfalls Emphasize appropriate graphing calculator use in Examples 6, 7, and 8: To prevent rounding error, use the built-in order of operations to evaluate expressions and enter the entire expression rather than doing the order of operations one step at a time.

Take several functions from Examples 2 and 3, as well as $y = x^3$ (linear, cubic or root) and ask the students to make tables and graphs (on graph paper) of the functions and their inverses. Make sure that the students observe the symmetry of the inverse functions. In groups, have students determine the new rule. Demonstrate how to find the rule using algebra. Have the students verify the rules they found by using algebra.

Power and root functions. Give a formal definition of power and root functions. Remind students of the domain restrictions on some root functions. After giving several examples of power and root functions, ask students to graph x cubed and the cube root of x on their calculators. Make sure that their viewing windows are "square."

Have the students practice finding inverse functions of root and power functions with Example 5 and with $y = \sqrt[4]{x}$.

Remind the students that the main purpose here was to solve equations. Explain the process needed to solve nth power and root equations, then have the students do Exercises 72 and 76, which have several square root equations. Do Exercise 35 for the class, then assign Exercises 64, 66, and 75 to be solved in groups.

Coaching for Homework (first day)

(5 minutes): (First day)Explain what is needed for Exercises 1 to 4 (just swap the x and y values). Remind students that they can check their solutions on their calculators by graphing both sides of the equations and looking for the x-values of the intersection points. If the students are encouraged to use their calculators, remind them to use parentheses where there is more than one term under a radical

Lecture/Group Activity (second day)

For the second day, do Exercise 82 with the class, then have students work on *Exercises 29, 34, 40, 44, 68, 71 and 77* in groups. Have the groups put problems on the board, showing all steps. Remind students to check their solutions.

Wrap-up. Going over the problems on the board is a good way to give closure to the class. Point out how inverse functions were used to solve the equations.

NOTE In the Review Exercises for Chapter 6, Exercise 44 is intended to practice multiplication of two-term expressions as well as properties of exponents and radicals. They have not appeared as homework exercises and are not appropriate for test items.

Section 7.0 Patterns, Geometric Sequences, and Exponential Equations

Preparation

Objectives

- Create tables and graphs, given activity settings or problem situations.
- Find the nth term, a_n, for a geometric sequence.
- Identify sequences created by linear, quadratic, or exponential functions that are restricted to positive integer inputs.
- Find the function of an exponential sequence with exponential regression.
- Show that the function and the nth term expression for a given sequence of numbers are equivalent.

Links

- Sequences: Sections 1.1, 2.4, 3.2, 4.1, Appendix 2.
- Regression: Sections 2.3, 4.1.
- Exponential functions: Section 7.1.

Time and Emphasis

50 minutes. Essential material.

Vocabulary

common ratio	exponential function	geometric sequence
nth term of a geometric sequence		quadratic sequence

Points to Stress

- Finding differences between terms permits us to identify linear, quadratic, and other sequences.
- Geometric sequences have differences that are either the same as or a multiple of the original sequence. However, they are not the only sequence with this pattern. A common ratio uniquely defines a geometric sequence.
- Any exponential function with the domain limited to the positive integers can be written as a geometric sequence.
- Use the properties of exponents to change exponential expressions b^{x+c} to ab^x, where $a = b^c$.

Suggested Lesson Format

Warm-up: 5 minutes

Questions on Homework: 10 minutes

Lecture/Group Activity: 25 minutes

Coaching for Homework: 5 minutes

Materials Needed for Class

Copies of *Exploring Patterns* (IRM page 116). Note: The questions on this worksheet are taken directly from Examples 1 and 2. A worksheet is provided here so the students can work on the problems without looking at the textbook.

Homework

Core exercises: 1 to 25, odd .

Sample assignment: 1 to 39, odd.

Optional Activities

The project in Exercise 48 shows sequences with differences similar to geometric but without the common ratios.

For Labs and Recitations

Do in pairs, Exercises 41 to 44

Bring a ball and collect experimental data for a bouncing ball situation like Example 2.

In Class

Warm-up

(5 minutes): Assign the Warm-up to be done individually.

Questions on Homework

(10 minutes): Have the students go over the homework in groups and select questions for class discussion.

Lecture/Group Activity

(25 minutes):

Introduction. It is natural for students to use differences to find the next number in a sequence so encourage them to check differences to identify the type of sequence and then move on to common ratios for geometric sequences in order to find the nth term, a_n.

> **NOTE**
>
> This and Section 7.1 begin with two application problems, one an increasing exponential function, the other a decreasing function. One application in each section lends itself to an in-class activity, the other is a "thinking activity". Together the four applications suggest the diversity of settings and similarity in functional behavior exhibited by exponential functions.

Activity. Motivate exponential functions and geometric sequences by having students work in groups of three to do the paper-folding activity and answer the questions on the super-ball bounces on the *Exploring Patterns* worksheet. Summarize by using differences to identify the functions as linear, quadratic, or neither.

Geometric sequences and exponential functions. To introduce geometric sequences, finding ratios, and the nth term of a geometric sequence, have groups write the nth term formula for Examples 1 and 2 and compare with their earlier results.

Define an exponential function and distinguish between it and geometric sequences, see Table 3 in the text.

Exponential regression. Apply exponential regression to the data from Examples 1 and 2 (Parts a and b of Example 7) and compare results with those from the nth term formula.

Use properties of exponents to show that the results from regression agree with the nth term formula. (Part a of Example 8).

Coaching for Homework

(5 minutes): *Exercises 23 to 36 are important practice in using properties of exponents. These skills will be used again in 7.1 to identify features in the graph of exponential functions.*

Exercises 41 to 44 remind us that not every geometric sequence can be changed to an exponential function. This helps us pay attention to conditions stated in the exponential function.

Exploring Patterns

Paper folding

   a. Fold a piece of paper in half. Then set up a table showing the number of times you folded as the input and the number of layers of paper created by the fold as the output. Fold the paper again and record the folds and layers. Continue folding the paper and recording the folds and layers until you get to the point where the paper is two thick to fold. Predict the number of layers you would create if you could fold the paper one more time.

   b. Graph the data from your table.

   c. Describe the number of layers of paper in terms of the number of folds you made.

   d. Is the pattern in the table and the graph an increasing or decreasing function?

Superball Bounces

   a. Suppose a superball bounces to $\frac{2}{3}$ of the height you dropped it from and $\frac{2}{3}$ of that height with each successive bounce. Suppose we drop the ball from a height of 108 inches. Make a table showing the heights of the first five bounces. Use 1 through 5 as the inputs and the heights of the ball as the outputs (consider drop from 108 inches as the height of the first bounce).

   b. Graph the data from your table.

   c. Describe the nth height of the ball.

   d. Is the pattern in the table and graph an increasing or a decreasing function?

Section 7.1 Exponential Functions and Graphs

Preparation

Objectives
- Identify the coefficient, the base, and the exponent in an exponential expression.
- Graph exponential functions.
- Examine how the base and coefficient of an exponential expression affect the graph of an exponential function.
- Identify the y-intercept for an exponential function.

Links
Exponential functions: Section 7.0.
Graphs: Section 7.3.

Time and Emphasis
50 minutes. Essential material.

Vocabulary
exponential function   horizontal asymptote

Points to Stress
- The coefficient a is the y-intercept of the graph of $y = ab^x$.
- If $0 < b < 1$, the graph of $y = bx$ decreases from left to right.
- If $b > 1$, the graph of $y = b^x$ increases from left to right.
- The domain for $f(x) = b^x$ is all real numbers.
- The range for $f(x) = b^x$ is $f(x) > 0$.
- The x-axis is a horizontal asymptote for $y = b^x$
- The graph of $y = b^x$ passes through $(0, 1)$ and $(1, b)$.

Suggested Lesson Format
Warm-up: 5 minutes
Questions on Homework: 10 minutes
Lecture/Group Activity: 25 minutes
Coaching for Homework: 5 minutes

Materials Needed for Class
Copies *Exploring More Patterns* (IRM page 119). Note: The questions on this worksheet are taken directly from Examples 1. A worksheet is provided here so the students can work on the problems without looking at the textbook.
A roll of 50 pennies, a sandwich bag, and a shallow box for each group.

Homework
Core exercises: 1 to 25, odd.
Sample assignment: 1 to 31, odd; 41, 43.

For Labs and Recitations
Do the project in Exercise 48 in pairs.

In Class

Warm-up

(5 minutes): Assign the Warm-up to be done individually.

Questions on Homework

(10 minutes): Have the students go over the homework in groups and select questions for class discussion.

Lecture/Group Activity

(25 minutes): Exponential functions. Assign *Exploring More Patterns* to be done in groups.

Discuss whether or not the results can be modeled with an exponential equation.

Repeat the definition of exponential function and discuss the conditions on its parameters and base. Assign Example 3 to be done in groups.

Exponential graphs. Have the students work in pairs using graphing calculators on the following exercises:

Graph and compare $y = 2^x$ and $y = (\frac{1}{2})^x$ (Example 4)

Graph and compare $y = 2^x$, $y = 3^x$, and $y = 4^x$. (Example 5)

As a whole class, discuss increasing, decreasing, and features such as points $(0, 1)$, $(1, b)$, horizontal asymptote.

Have the students work in pairs to graph and compare $f(x) = 1 \bullet 2^x$, $f(x) = 5 \bullet 2^x$, $f(x) = 10 \bullet 2^x$ (Example 8)

Discuss the y-intercepts.

If horizontal shifts are included in your curriculum, do Examples 6 and 7 and Exercises 31 to 37.

Coaching for Homework

(5 minutes): *Exercises 19 to 24 are similar to exercises in Section 7.0. In Exercises 19 to 21, write the coefficient a as a power of the base and use the properties of exponents to change the equations.*

Exercises 39 and 40 require careful reasoning about exponential equations and their graphs.

Exercises 41 to 44 explore equations that look exponential but may not be.

Section 7.2 Solving Exponential Equations: Like Bases and Logarithms

Preparation

Objectives
- Use like bases to solve exponential equations.
- Find the inverse to an exponential function by table, graph, and equation.
- Change between exponential equations and logarithmic equations.
- Evaluate common logarithms with a calculator.

Links
- Inverse functions: Section 6.4.
- Common logarithms: Section 7.3.
- Solving equations: Section 7.4.

Time and Emphasis
50 minutes. Essential material.

Vocabulary
common logarithm	like bases property
logarithm	logarithmic function

Points to Stress
- To use the like bases property, change the exponential expressions on both sides of an equation to the same base, set the exponents equal, and solve for the variable.

- The logarithmic function, $y = \log_b x$, is the inverse function to the exponential function, $y = b^x$, $b > 0$, $b \neq 1$, $x \geq 0$.

- The equations $y = b^x$ and $x = \log_b y$ are equivalent.

- The base b for an equivalent pair of exponential and logarithmic equations is the same.

Suggested Lesson Format
Warm-up: 5 minutes

Questions on Homework: 10 minutes

Lecture/Group Activity: 25 minutes

Coaching for Homework: 5 minutes

Materials Needed for Class

Homework
<u>Core exercises</u>: 1 to 17, odd; 25 to 33, odd; 43 to 48, odd.

<u>Sample assignment</u>: 1 to 55, odd; 63.

For Labs and Recitations

Assign Exercises 19 to 24, and 51 to 57 to be done in groups of three.

In Class

Warm-up

(5 minutes): Assign the Warm-up to be done individually.

Questions on Homework

(10 minutes): Have the students go over the homework in groups and select questions for class discussion.

Lecture/Group Activity

(25 minutes): Introduction. Explain to the class that we can solve exponential equations by tables and graphs, guess and check, or with two new methods introduced in this section: like bases and logarithms.

Like bases. Return to the Warm-up and have pairs of students write, if possible, the number on the right side of each equation as a power of the base on the left side.

Introduce the like bases property and use it to show the solutions to all equations except equation 3, which we will solve below, and equation 7, which we will solve in the next section.

Have students apply the like bases property to solving the equations from Example 2.

Logarithms. Explain to the class that two of the equations in the Warm-up could not be solved with like bases. For these equations, $10^x = 20$ and $2^x = 6$, we need the inverse operation to the exponential function in order to solve for x.

Return to the material in Section 6.4 and have pairs of students find the inverse function to $y = 10^x$ by table, graph, and with algebra (if possible). (Examples 3, 4, and 5).

Define the inverse function.

Define the logarithm (the box on page 499).

Use the definition of the logarithm to complete the table in Example 6.

> *Journal Entry* Table 9 and Table 13 provide practice in changing between exponential and logarithmic form and a visual reminder to associate these two functions. I refer to this as "using the definition of logarithms to solve the equations". —AK

Evaluating logarithms.

Use the calculator to evaluate base 10 logarithms (Example 7 and Example 8). It is okay to have students look at the book for Example 8 because they will see immediately if they are using their calculators correctly.

Have students work in pairs on Example 9 to observe numbers for which finding the logarithm with a calculator does not work. Summarize the results from this example by returning to the definition of the Logarithmic Function, page 498, and observing the restrictions on x and b.

Coaching for Homework

(5 minutes): *After changing the equations in Exercises 41 and 42 to logarithmic equations, use a calculator to find x. Remember, log base 10 on the calculator is the [LOG] key.*

Additional examples for solving the logarithmic equations in Exercises 43 to 48 are shown in Example 10. Note that the x is in a variety of locations in the equations, including the base. Keep in mind restrictions on the base and on the input to the logarithmic function.

Section 7.3 Applications of Exponential and Logarithmic Functions

Preparation

Objectives (Day One)
- Identify the base for a common logarithm.
- Change equations between exponential and logarithmic form to solve pH and Richter scale problems.
- Apply the change of base formula to evaluate logarithms.
- Graph logarithmic functions on a calculator.

Links
- Graphs: Section 7.1.
- Common logarithms: Section 7.2.
- Change of base formula: Section 7.4.

Time and Emphasis
50 minutes. Essential material. Day of one of two days.

Vocabulary
change of base formula   common logarithm

Points to Stress

- Common, or base 10, logarithms are written without the base: $\log_{10} x = \log x$.
- In order to change $y = ab^x$ to an equivalent logarithmic equation, divide both sides by a.
- The change of base formula may be written with any base. Base 10 is usually convenient. Use the change of base formula to calculator graphs of logarithms with bases other than 10.
- Graphs of logarithmic functions $y = \log_b x$ or $b^y = x$ pass through the x-intercept $(1, 0)$ because $b^0 = 1$ and pass through $(b, 1)$ because $b^1 = b$.
- Graphs of logarithmic functions have no y-intercept because $y = \log_b 0$ is undefined.

Suggested Lesson Format
Warm-up: 5 minutes
Questions on Homework: 10 minutes
Lecture/Group Activity: 25 minutes
Coaching for Homework: 5 minutes

Materials Needed for Class
None

Optional Activity
The Birthday Gift Option project in Exercise 67 is an ideal summary of the term because it illustrates three different functions, none of which are "obvious" to the student. You might try this problem next term as an introduction to the course. Option 2 in the project raises interesting rounding questions.

Homework
Core exercises: 1, 3, 7, 11, 13, 17 to 21, odd; 23, 25, 27, 29.

Sample assignment: 1 to 31, odd.

For Labs and Recitations
Have students work in pairs to make tables and graphs:
For the exponential functions use inputs $x = -3$ to $x = 3$.
Show (with algebra and definition of a logarithm) that the given logarithmic function is the inverse function to the exponential function.
Next, reverse x and y in the table for the exponential function and use this new table to graph the logarithmic function.

1. $y = 2^x$, $y = \log_2 x$
2. $y = 3^x$, $y = \log_3 x$
3. $y = 4^{(-x)}$, $y = -\log_4 x$
4. $y = 2^{x+1}$, $y = -1 + \log_2 x$
5. $y = 3^{x-1}$, $y = 1 + \log_3 x$

In checking with a graphing calculator, use the change of base formula within the equation containing a logarithm. For example, $\log_2 x$ should be written $\log (x)/\log(2)$.

In Class

Warm-up
(5 minutes):
Questions on Homework
(10 minutes):
Lecture/Group Activity
(25 minutes): The warm-up returns to material from Section 7.2 and provides a transition to applications with common logarithms. These applications use standard logarithmic notation and do not show the base; hence, we must introduce the notation $\log_{10} x = \log x$.

Applications. Stress recognition of base 10 and manipulation of formulas rather than details of the applications themselves.

Work Examples 2, 3, and 5 with the class.

Change of base formula. Remind students that we were not able to solve $2^x = 6$ in Section 7.2 because we could not evaluate $\log_2 6$. The change of base formula does this. Have students work in pairs on Example 6.

Graphing logarithmic functions. Have students work in pairs using the table and graph on the graphing calculator to compare the graphs of $y = \log_2 x$ and $y = \log_5 x$.

> **NOTE** Reminder to Students and Instructors
> When entering the change of base formula on the calculator, remember to always enter the closing parentheses on the log function.

Summarize the properties of the logarithmic graph (pages 510 to 511).

Coaching for Homework(5 minutes): *Remember that logarithms without a base are base 10. To improve understanding and to prevent errors, fill in the base every time you write a logarithmic expression.*

Extension question: *In Exercises 17 to 20, look for patterns in the logarithms of numbers with the same base and the same decimal part.*

[Note to instructor: The following is a sample answer to the extension question. The logarithms, base 2, of 3, 6, 12, and 24 all have 0.58 as the decimal part. Each of these numbers is a 3 times a power of 2. The exponent on 2 controls the number before the decimal and $\log_2 3$ gives 1.58 and controls the decimal part.

A similar pattern holds for the logarithms, base 2, of 5, 10, and 20, where each is 5 times a power of 2; the logarithms, base 3, of 2, 6, and 18, where each is 2 times a power of 3; the logarithms, base 3, of 4 and 12; the logarithms, base 5, of 2 and 10; the logarithms, base 5, of 6 and 30; the logarithms, base 4 of 3 and 12; and the logarithms, base 4, of 5 and 20.]

Section 7.3 Applications of Exponential and Logarithmic Functions

Preparation

Objectives (Day Two)
- Solve applications with compound interest and exponential growth and decay.
- Estimate doubling time with the rule of 72.

Links (Day Two)
- Compound interest: Sections 6.1, 6.4, 7.5.
- Calculator regression: Section 7.0.

Time and Emphasis
Day two of two days. 50 minutes. Optional material.

Vocabulary (Day Two)

doubling time	exponential decay	exponential growth
half-life	rule of 72	

Points to Stress
- The change of base formula permits solving for time in the compound interest formula.
- Two special forms of compound interest are the time it takes for money to double (doubling time) and the time for a object to drop to half its original value (half-life).
- The rule of 72 gives a way to estimate doubling time for interest compounded annually.
- We can fit an exponential regression to data and find the annual rate of growth (or decline).

Suggested Lesson Format

Warm-up: 5 minutes

Questions on Homework: 10 minutes

Lecture/Group Activity: 25 minutes

Coaching for Homework: 5 minutes

Materials Needed for Class

None

Optional Activity

Do research on the Internet and find either the current doubling time or the current population growth rates for Kenya, Brazil, India, and China. Compare these to the data in Exercises 45 and 46. Use your data to find the missing data, either the doubling time or annual growth rate.

Watch exponential growth on the graphing calculator with a recursion formula. Suppose the initial population is 100 people and the population is growing 3% each year. The recursion process is

100 [ENTER]

[ANS] + 0.06 × [ANS][ENTER]

Repeat [ENTER] to obtain successive results

Homework

Core exercises: 33 to 39, odd; 41, 45, 47, 53, 61.

Sample assignment: 33 to 47, 53, 55, 59, 61.

For Labs and Recitations

Repeat the penny toss activity in Section 7.2, Example 1. Discuss the results in terms of exponential growth and decay:

1. Will the growth rate be positive or negative? [Answer: Negative, the number of pennies declines.]
2. What do we expect the growth rate to be? [Answer: 50%]
3. What is the theoretical equation for starting with 48 pennies? [Answer: $y = 48(0.50)^x$]
4. How does the exponential regression equation compare with the theoretical equation?
5. What is the half-life for the penny toss? [Answer: Because the rate is 50%, the half-life is one toss.]

In Class

Warm-up

(5 minutes): Assign the Warm-up to be done individually.

Questions on Homework

(10 minutes): Have the students go over the homework in groups and select questions for class discussion.

Lecture/Group Activity

(25 minutes): More applications.

We return to compound interest to find other applications of the change of base formula, solving for time, including doubling time and half-life.

Have students, in pairs, set up the annual compound interest formula for Example 9 and then solve it with the change of base formula.

Write these summaries for students:

> **NOTE** The topics of exponential growth and decay are usually based on continuous compounding and require the natural number, e, and natural logarithm, $\ln x$. Growth is modeled here with annual growth rates so as to introduce students to this very important topic with a minimum of mathematics. Informed citizens must understand the basic principles of this topic.

- Doubling time implies that the ending amount, S, is twice the initial amount P.

- Substitute $2P$ for S in the compound interest formula. Substitute the other information.

- Solving for t then gives the doubling time.

- Half-life implies that the ending amount, S, is half the initial amount P.

- Substitute $\frac{1}{2}P$ for S in the compound interest formula. Substitute the other information.

- Solving for t then gives the half-life.

Continue with students setting up the equations for Examples 10 and 12.

Using regression equations to find the growth (or decay) rate, r is given in Example 14.

This is optional material but useful in helping students relate the regression equations to the compound interest formula. Because inflation (or rarely, deflation) are discussed in the news, students should see how they can take data and calculate the growth (or decay) rate for themselves.

Try to obtain these calculator exponential regression summaries from the students:

An exponential equation with rate of growth r has 1 + r as a base. If the base is greater than one, subtract 1 to find r.

An exponential equation with rate of decay (decline) -r has 1 - r as a base. Thus if the base is less than one, subtract the base from 1 to find r.

Coaching for Homework

(5 minutes): *In Exercises 37 to 40, think about the annual compound interest formula,*

$S = P(1 + r)t.$

NOTE The projects in Exercises 66 and 67 contain three options for students to evaluate, write equations, and decide which gives the best results. Here is a two-option scenario.

Weekly Allowance Plan: Your young daughter's allowance is $1 per week. After visiting her grandmother (a mathematics teacher) she returns home with a new year's proposal: $0.01 the first week and doubling each week thereafter. What do you think of her proposal? In how many weeks will the two allowance methods be equal? In how many weeks will the total received be equal? What will happen to your family budget?

Section 7.4 Properties of Logarithms and the Logarithmic Scale

Preparation

Objectives
- Prove the properties of logarithms.
- Apply properties of logarithms in writing expressions.
- Solve equations by taking the logarithm of both sides.
- Prove the change of base formula.
- Read a logarithmic scale.
- Graph data on semilog graph paper.

Links
- Solving exponential equations: Section 7.2.
- Change of Base Formula: Section 7.3.

Time and Emphasis
50 minutes. Optional material.

Vocabulary

logarithmic scale   semilog graph

Points to Stress

- Because logarithms are exponents, the properties of exponents have parallel interpretations in the properties of logarithms.

- Once we have the property $\log_b (m \bullet n) = \log_b m + \log_b n$, we can derive the other properties of logarithms.

- The graph of an exponential function becomes a straight line on semilog graph paper.

Suggested Lesson Format

Warm-up: 5 minutes

Questions on Homework: 10 minutes

Lecture/Group Activity: 25 minutes

Coaching for Homework: 5 minutes

Materials Needed for Class

Copies of semilog graph paper on page 527.

Optional Activity

The project on Antilogs in Exercise 57.

Homework

Core exercises: 3 to 37, odd; 41, 53.

Sample assignment: 1 to 43, odd; 45 to 50, all; 53.

> **NOTE**
> In many curricula, properties of logarithms are delayed until college algebra. Spending extra time on the material in Sections 7.1 to 7.3 is thought to benefit students more in the long run than continuing on to properties and solving equations by taking the logarithm of both sides.

For Labs and Recitations

Assign the project on Scientific Notation and Logarithms in Exercise 56.

In Class

Warm-up

(5 minutes): Assign the Warm-up to be done individually.

Questions on Homework

(10 minutes): Have the students go over the homework in groups and select questions for class discussion.

Lecture/Group Activity

(25 minutes): Properties of logarithms. Looking for patterns in Exercises 17 to 20 in Section 7.3 as well as looking for patterns in the Warm-up can lead students to recognizing the product property of logarithms (see Examples 3, 4, and 5).

Prove the product property by doing Example 1 as a class. Ask students to work in pairs on Example 2 to suggest how to prove the power property. Leave the quotient property as an exercise.

Solving equations. Do Example 6 with the class to review solving an exponential equation with like bases and another equation with the definition of the logarithm. With the class do Example 7, where the equations are repeated and solved by taking the logarithm of both sides. Do Example 8 with the class to prove the change of base formula is an application of taking the logarithm of both sides of an equation.

Logarithmic scale (optional). If time allows, explain to the class that countless illustrations in science, forestry, medical, and technical publications employ a logarithmic scale on one or both axes. The motivation for the logarithmic scale is that it permits widely spaced numbers to be shown on the same axis. Distribute semilog graph paper (vertical axis is logarithmic) to students and have them work individually to graph $y = 2^x$ and compare the results with that on normal axes as done in Example 9 and Example 10. Have the students read Example 11. Offer extra credit for students who bring in photocopies (with source notations) of logarithmic graphs.

Coaching for Homework

(5 minutes): *The directions to Exercises 23 to 38 are at the bottom of the first column at the bottom of page 527.*

Section 7.5 The Natural Number *e* in Exponential and Logarithmic Functions

Preparation

Objectives
- Calculate the powers and roots of *e*.
- Apply the formula for continuously compounded interest.
- Find logarithms for base *e*.
- Change natural logarithmic equations to exponential equations and solve.
- Change exponential equations to natural logarithmic equations and solve.

Links
- Compound interest: Sections 6.1, 6.4, 7.3.
- Doubling time: Section 7.3.
- Rule of 72: Section 7.3

Time and Emphasis
50 minutes. Optional material.

Vocabulary

continuously compounded interest	*e*, the natural number	factorial
natural logarithm	rule of 69	

Points to Stress

- The formula $S = Pe^{rt}$ is used whenever interest is compounded continuously.

- The logarithms with base *e*, $\log_e x$, are usually written, with calculator key [LN].

- When working with logarithmic expressions involving either base 10 or base *e*, rewrite the expressions to show the base.

Suggested Lesson Format

Warm-up: 5 minutes

Questions on Homework: 10 minutes

Lecture/Group Activity: 25 minutes

Coaching for Homework: 5 minutes

Materials Needed for Class

None

Homework

Core exercises: 1 to 27, odd

Sample assignment: 1 to 43, odd; 47

For Labs and Recitations

Practice graphing with e^x and $\ell n\, x$ in the project in Exercise 48.

In Class

Warm-up

(5 minutes): Assign the Warm-up to be done individually.

Questions on Homework

(10 minutes): Have the students go over the homework in groups and select questions for class discussion.

Lecture/Group Activity

(25 minutes): Compound interest. Have students work in pairs on the compound interest problem posed in Example 1. Ask the pairs to suggest what will happen when the number of compoundings is $n = 5000$.

Discuss the limit approached by increasing the number of compoundings, see Figure 21 in the text.

The natural number. Place $(1 + 1/x)^x$ in [$y =$] on a calculator and use the table to evaluate for progressively larger inputs, see Example 2
Calculating with e. Have students work in pairs on Example 3.

Define continuously compounded interest and do Parts a and c from Example 5.

Logarithms, base e. Solve Example 7 and Example 8 to introduce the advantage of having the logarithm, base e, on the calculator.

Use Example 9 to motivate using tables for changing between exponential and logarithmic equations. Have students complete Table 18 in pairs.

Coaching for Homework

(5 minutes): *For Exercises 25 and 32 refer to Example 11, the rule of 69 (like the rule of 72 in Section 7.3).*

For Exercises 37 to 40, refer to Examples 12 and 13 and review changing from logarithmic to exponential form.

Section 8.0 Solving Systems of Equations by Substitution and Elimination

Preparation

Objectives

Solve problems by guess and check.

Write a system of equations using information obtained by guess and check.

Find the solutions to a system of linear equations by substitution and elimination.

Solve application problems.

Links

Guess and check: Section 2.0.

Roadbed transition curves: Section 4.5.

Time and Emphasis

50 minutes. Essential material.

Vocabulary

elimination method	in terms of
solution to the system	standard form of a linear equation
substitution method	system of equations

Points to Stress

Guess and check provides a way to build equations in unfamiliar settings.

Steps in solving equations by substitution.

Steps in solving equations by elimination

Suggested Lesson Format

Warm-up: 5 minutes

Questions on Homework: 10 minutes

Lecture/Group Activity: 25 minutes

Coaching for Homework: 5 minutes

Materials Needed for Class

None

Homework

Core exercises: 23 to 43, odd; 45, 47.

Sample assignment: 1 to 55, odd.

For Labs and Recitations

Roadbed transition curves. We return to the transition curve parabolic model, Section 4.5. The additional fact needed to find the equation of the roadbed is the slope of the roadbed at any point x: $m = 2ax + b$. This slope changes from point to point whereas the slope of a line is constant. Discuss Example 11. Work in pairs on Exercises 53 to 56. The process lends itself to a spreadsheet as suggested in the project in Exercise 57.

In Class

Warm-up

(5 minutes): Assign the Warm-up to be done individually.

Questions on Homework

(10 minutes): Have the students go over the homework in groups and select questions for class discussion.

Lecture/Group Activity

(25 minutes): Guess and check. Begin by explaining to the class that we return to the guess and check skills introduced in Section 2.0. Many of the hardest word problems can be understood or even solved by guess and check. The bonus is that the guess and check process helps in writing equations.

Lead the students through Example 1, suggesting someone's birth date as a starting number. Consider the solution to a word problem to be a separate topic from writing equations for a word problem. Have pairs of students try a problem such as Exercise 4.

Substitution method. Explain to the class that when we solved formulas for a letter we were writing that letter in terms of the other variables. We stress "in terms of" here and first practice solving a two-variable equation for one variable.

Have students solve the system of equations in Example 4 by substitution. Discuss what makes an exercise reasonable to do by substitution.

Return to the system of equations generated in Example 1 and solve by substitution.

Elimination method. Return to the warm-up and discuss how the warm-up suggests the validity of adding equal quantities to each side of an equation.

In order to have a useful result from addition, that is, eliminating one variable from the system, we write the equations in standard form. Define the standard form of a linear equation, page 556, and point out that this form includes vertical lines, $x = c$, which are not linear functions and cannot be written with $y = mx + b$.

Lead the class through Example 8, where no multiplication is needed and then have pairs of students do Example 9 where one multiplication is needed. Discuss the need to multiply both equations by constants to obtain opposite terms that will add to zero and have pairs of students do Example 10.

Coaching for Homework

(5 minutes): *In Exercises 1 to 6, stress finding the solution with guess and check and then using the guess and check table to build a system of equations.*

Use elimination on Exercises 49 and 50. Look carefully for terms that may be made into opposites by multiplying one equation by –1. To isolate one variable (x or y) you will need to factor one side after adding (or subtracting) the equations.

126

Section 8.1 Solving Systems of Two Linear Equations by Graphing

Preparation   **Objectives**
- Solve systems of linear equations by graphing.
- Identify systems of two linear equations having a single solution, an infinite number of solutions, or no solution.
- Explain the algebraic results from solving systems containing equations whose graphs are parallel or coincident.
- Solve quantity and value problems by writing and solving systems of equations.

Links
Solving by graphing: Section 2.0 and 2.2.
Special cases: Section 8.2.

Time and Emphasis
50 minutes. Essential material.

Vocabulary

coincident lines	parallel lines	per	quantity
quantity-value table	value		

Points to Stress
- Every point on the graph of an equation makes the equation true.
- The point of intersection of two graphs is the ordered pair that makes both equations true.
- A true statement, such as $0 = 0$, in the solution to a system of equations implies that there are an infinite number of solutions. In the case of graphs of two linear equations in two variables, the lines are coincident.
- A false statement, such as $0 = 1$, in the solution to a system of equations implies that there are no real-number solutions. In the case of graphs of two linear equations in two variables, the lines are parallel.
- Many problem situations have more than one number describing a given item. These different numbers can often be described by quantity and value. Quantity-value tables help us organize information when solving word problems.

Suggested Lesson Format
Warm-up: 5 minutes
Questions on Homework: 10 minutes
Lecture/Group Activity: 25 minutes
Coaching for Homework: 5 minutes

Materials Needed for Class
Transparency of *Solutions to Systems of Two Linear Equations* (IRM page 132).

Homework
Core exercises: 1 to 11, odd; 13 to 33, every other odd.
Sample assignment: 1 to 11, odd; 13 to 43, every other odd.

For Labs and Recitations
Examine the role of *a*, *b*, and *c* in the graph of linear equations with the project in Exercise 45. Do the exercise in groups of three.

In Class

Warm-up

(5 minutes): Assign the Warm-up to be done in groups.

Questions on Homework

(10 minutes): Have the students go over the homework in groups and select questions for class discussion.

Lecture/Group Activity

(25 minutes):

Solve a system of equations by graphing. Graph the system of equations in Example 1 and discuss finding the point of intersection as the solution to the equations. (Review question: Are the lines perpendicular?)

Graph the system of equations in Examples 2 and 3. Solve the systems, if possible.

Solve the systems with substitution or elimination. Discuss the results.

Summarize coincident lines and parallel lines.

Have groups copy and complete the table from the transparency *Solutions to Systems of Two Linear Equations* (taken from Table 3 on page 567).

Quantity-value tables. Explain to the class that facts in a word problem are frequently identified as quantity (how many) or value (monetary worth or rate). Quantity-value tables permit us to organize information. Then, if we pay attention to units, we can see how the facts relate to each other.

Have students identify quantity and value in Examples 6 and 7, then set up tables to solve the problems.

Coaching for Homework

(5 minutes): *Notice that Exercises 13 to 18 only request that you identify the quantity and value for each setting. No problem needs to be solved.*

In Exercises 19 to 22, there is missing information that is assumed to be common knowledge. Here also make up a question that might be asked.

Solutions to Systems of Two Linear Equations

Arrange the following information the table below to summarize solutions to two linear equations.

The variables drop out and the remaining statement is false.

An infinite number of ordered pairs satisfy the system.

One ordered pair is the solution.

The equations can be solved for x and y.

There is no real-number solution to the system.

The variables drop out and the remaining statement is true.

Geometry	Intersecting lines	Coincident lines	Parallel lines
Algebra			
Solution			

Section 8.2 Solving Systems of Two Linear Equations with Matrices

Preparation

Objectives (Day One)
- Use a calculator to solve a matrix equation, if a solution exists.
- Use algebra and/or graphing calculator to find whether a system without a unique solution represents parallel or coincident lines.

Links
- Standard form of a linear equation: Section 8.0.
- Solving a system of equations: Sections 8.1 and 8.3.

Time and Emphasis

Day One of two: 50 minutes. Essential material (for Section 8.3)

Day Two of two: 50 minutes. Optional material, if you emphasize the matrix theory.

Vocabulary (Day One)

Use the vocabulary correctly in this section but define it carefully in Day 2.

determinant

matrix	matrix equation	matrix inverse
matrix of coefficients	matrix of constants	matrix of variables
shape of a matrix		

Points to Stress

- The elimination method for two linear equations can be generalized to any equation, similarly, matrices permit us to solve any linear system of equations, if a unique solution exists.
- Writing the linear equations in standard form is essential (as in writing $ax^2 + bx + c = 0$ to find a, b, and c for using the quadratic formula.

> **NOTE**
> Two other matrix procedures, Cramer's rule and row-reduced echelon form, are not presented here. The availability of matrix operations on the calculator makes Cramer's rule obsolete. Row-reduction operations are available on most calculators and may be introduced separately if desired...but it is recommended that they be delayed until college algebra.

Suggested Lesson Format

Warm-up: 5 minutes

Questions on Homework: 5 minutes

Lecture/Group Activity: 35 minutes

Coaching for Homework: 5 minutes

Materials Needed for Class

Overhead calculator.

Homework

Core exercises: 35 to 41, odd; 45 to 49, odd.

Sample assignment: 35 to 51, odd.

> **For Labs and Recitations**
> See Preparation for Day Two of this Section.

In Class   **Warm-up**

(5 minutes): Assign the Warm-up to be done individually.

Questions on Homework

(10 minutes): Have the students go over the homework in groups and select questions for class discussion.

Lecture/Group Activity

(25 minutes): Students are highly motivated to have the calculator solve systems of equations. Explain that matrices permit solving systems of linear equations, $ax + by = c$ and $dx + ey = f$, in a similar way as the quadratic formula solves equations $ax^2 + bx + c = 0$. We must write the equations into a certain form and then correctly enter the coefficient data into the calculator.

Explain that you will go through the complete procedure three times during this class and at least once again during the next class. The students should be patient with themselves and just follow along as far as they can on each example. As students catch on, have them team up with someone who doesn't understand. Don't try to get everyone to understand the first, or even the second example.

Introduce the procedure with one problem, Example 7. It takes 20 minutes to do the example and follow the chart on page 579. Set up the system on the chalkboard and have a student work the overhead calculator. Other students should work in pairs on one calculator.

Do a second example, say Exercise 29 in Section 8.0, with students working in pairs along with you on their own calculators—this takes 10 minutes.

Do a third example, Exercise 31 in Section 8.0, taking about 5 minutes.

In the next class introduce the theory, see Day 2.

Coaching for Homework

(5 minutes): *Set up solutions to the systems with the calculator matrices. If det[A] = 0, you must stop and solve the equations by hand to find out whether the systems have no solution or an infinite number of solutions. Note whether the graphs of the equations will be parallel or coincident.*

For Exercise 51 let x and y be the variables, write a system, and solve it on the calculator. Round answers to the nearest whole number.

Section 8.2 Solving Systems of Two Linear Equations with Matrices

Preparation

Objectives (Day Two)
- Multiply matrices by hand and with a calculator.
- Find the determinant of a matrix by hand and with a calculator.
- Translate a system of linear equations into a matrix equation.
- Use the determinant to identify systems of linear equations with a unique solution.

Links (Day Two)
- Standard form of a linear equation: Section 8.0.
- Solving a system of equations: Sections 8.1 and 8.3.

Time and Emphasis
Day two of two: 50 minutes. Optional material.

Vocabulary (Day Two)

determinant	identity matrix	matrix
matrix equation	matrix inverse	matrix of coefficients
matrix of constants	matrix of variables	shape of a matrix
square matrix		

Points to Stress
- Know the conditions for when two matrices can be added.
- Know the conditions for when a matrix can have an inverse.

Suggested Lesson Format
Warm-up: 5 minutes
Questions on Homework: 10 minutes
Lecture/Group Activity: 25 minutes
Coaching for Homework: 5 minutes

Materials Needed for Class
None

Optional Activity
There are several limitations on matrix multiplication that are not mentioned here. For example, can all matrices be multiplied? [no] How do we tell if matrices can be multiplied? [Find shape: $r_1 \times c_1 \bullet r_2 \times c_2$, the middle c_1 and r_2 must be the same number and the answer is the outer numbers $r_1 \bullet c_2$.]

Homework
Core exercises: 1 to 13, odd; 23, 25, 29, 33 a, 53 to 59, odd.
Sample assignment: 1 to 13, odd; 23, 25, 29, 33, 46, 48, 50, 53 to 59, odd.

For Labs and Recitations
Explore multiplication of two 2 by 2 matrices by having pairs of students do Exercises 18 to 24.
Discuss whether all multiplication of matrices is commutative. [Answer: Multiplication is not commutative.]
What is one matrix product that is commutative? [Answer: The product of $[A]$ and $[A]^{-1}$ is the same as $[A]^{-1}$ and $[A]$.]

In Class

Warm-up

(5 minutes): Set up matrices for the system of equations given in Exercises 10, 11, and 12 from Section 8.1.

Questions on Homework

(10 minutes): Have the students go over the homework in groups and select questions for class discussion.

Lecture/Group Activity

(25 minutes): Addition and Subtraction. Give students two matrices of the same shape and ask them to guess how the matrices might be added or subtracted. Do the addition and subtraction. Pose the question to the class: *How does the elimination method of adding equations suggest that we add terms in the same position?*

> **TIP**
> When multiplying matrices, it may be helpful to place two adjacent fingers on the first numbers being multiplied, then move the fingers to match the next two numbers being multiplied. An across-the-row times down-the-column pattern will become apparent.

Multiplication. Stress that the left side of a system of linear equations in standard form, the $ax + by$ and $cx + dy$ is precisely the product of the matrices $[A]$ and $[X]$ below.

$$[A] = \begin{bmatrix} a & b \\ c & d \end{bmatrix} \qquad [X] = \begin{bmatrix} x \\ y \end{bmatrix}$$

Do Example 1a with the class.

Explain that to multiply two 2-by-2 matrices we use the prior product twice, once for each column of the second matrix. Do Example 2 with the class and then Part b of Example 3.

Identities and inverses. Define the identity and inverse matrices based on the outcome of Part b in Example 3. Enter matrix $[A]$ into the calculator and find its inverse matrix. Compare it with that given in Example 3. Enter the inverse of $[A]$ into matrix $[B]$ and take its inverse to get back to $[A]$.

Determinants. Write the matrix equation from the third Warm-up exercise (Section 8.1, Exercise 12). Identify the matrix of coefficients $[A]$, matrix of variables $[X]$, and matrix of constants $[B]$. Calculate the determinant of the coefficient matrix A by hand. Because the determinant is not zero we may solve the matrix equation, $[A][X] = [B]$ for A by multiplying on the left of both sides by the inverse of $[A]$, obtaining $[X] = [A]^{-1}[B]$.

Repeat for the matrix equation from the first warm-up exercise (Section 8.1, Exercise 10). Identify the matrix of coefficients, matrix of variables, and matrix of constants. Calculate the determinant of the coefficient matrix A by hand and observe that the determinant is zero. In this case we must stop and solve by hand to find whether the system of two linear equations has no solutions (parallel lines) or an infinite number of solutions (coincident lines).

Coaching for Homework

(5 minutes): *In Exercises 53 to 56, use a quantity-value table with x = quantity of one strength solution and y = quantity of the other strength solution. The blend is considered the total. Remember to write the percents as decimals.*

Section 8.3 Matrix Solutions of Systems of Three or More Linear Equations

Preparation

Objectives

- Identify a graphical system as containing graphs of consistent, inconsistent, or dependent equations.
- Solve a system of three or more equations with matrices on a calculator.
- Describe possible implications of a zero determinant.
- Set up and solve systems of equations for applications.

Links

- Solving systems of equations: Sections 8.0, 8.1, and 8.2.
- Special cases: Section 8.1.
- Matrices: Section 8.2.

Time and Emphasis

50 minutes. Optional material.

Vocabulary

consistent equations	degree 1	dependent equations
inconsistent equations	linear equations	ordered triples
planes		

Points to Stress

- We generalize the definition of linear equations to multiple variables.
- The graphs of linear equations of two variables, $ax + by = c$, describe lines.
- The graphs of linear equations of three variables, $ax + by + cz = d$ describe planes.
- There is no graphical interpretation for linear equations of four or more variables.
- If a system of linear equations has exactly one solution, the system is consistent.
- The determinant of a matrix for a consistent system is nonzero.
- If the determinant is zero, the system is either inconsistent or dependent. A system of equations is inconsistent if it has no solution. A system of equations is dependent if it has an infinite number of solutions.
- Solve inconsistent or dependent systems by hand.

Suggested Lesson Format

Warm-up: 5 minutes

Questions on Homework: 10 minutes

Lecture/Group Activity: 25 minutes

Coaching for Homework: 5 minutes

Materials Needed for Class

Transparency of Systems of Three Linear Equations (IRM page 140). Note: This transparency is based on Table 7 on page 590.

Homework

Core exercises: 3 to 13, odd.

Sample assignment: 1 to 23, odd, 32.

For Labs and Recitations

Have students pick five arbitrary points on a rectangular coordinate grid and find a fourth-degree polynomial that passes through the points as in Example 9. This practices solving a system of five equations with a 5-by-5 coefficient matrix. There is an important teacher's note beside this example citing the subtle difference between solving for variables (Examples 7 and 8) and solving for coefficients (Example 9). When we solve for the variables we need n equations to find n unknowns. When we solve for coefficients, we need $n + 1$ equations because of the constant term.

In Class

Warm-up

(5 minutes): Assign the following exercise from Example 3 to be done individually. Solve by substitution: $a + b + c = 3$, $2a + 3b + c = 13$, $2a - b = 0$

Questions on Homework

(10 minutes): Have the students go over the homework in groups and select questions for class discussion.

Lecture/Group Activity

(25 minutes): Linear equations: Systems of linear equations in more than two variables. Begin by defining linear equations. Then examine various intersections of sets of three planes and resulting number of solutions. Define consistent, inconsistent, and dependent equations.

Solving systems of three equations. Have students, in pairs, set up matrices for the system in the warm-up (Example 3). Discuss the shape of the matrices. Evaluate the determinant of the coefficients matrix and find the solution to the system.

Inconsistent systems and dependent systems of equations. Have students, in pairs, set up matrices for Examples 4 and 5 and show that both give a zero determinant for the matrix of coefficients.

Have students copy the blank Table 7 from the transparency of *Systems of Three Linear Equations* and then complete the table given the facts.

> **TIP** Use the classroom or other objects to examine how three plane surfaces relate to each other.
> - The floor and two walls may meet at a corner point, a unique solution.
> - Three floors of a multi-story building are parallel and have no solution.
> - The floor, ceiling and one wall of a room also have no common solution.
> - Three planes may intersect in a line as in the pages of an open book.
> - Three planes may intersect, but not in a unique line as in the sides of a Toblerone candy box. The ends of the box are planes that intersect two other planes in a single point.

Do one application setting of interest as time permits.

Coaching for Homework

(5 minutes): *In Exercises 15 to 22, define the variables carefully. In Exercise 15, p might be the number of grams of protein not p = protein.*

Exercises 25 to 29 expand on the chocolate store setting in Examples 7 and 8 and extend it to matrix multiplication.

Systems of Three Linear Equations

Complete the table with these statements:

The variables drop out, and the resulting statement is false.

There is linear or planar intersection.

There is no solution.

There is one solution, an ordered triple.

Planes intersect in one common point.

The variables drop out, and the resulting statement is true.

There is no common intersection.

Equations can be solved to yield unique x, y, and z values.

An infinite number of ordered triples satisfy the system.

Systems of Three Linear Equations	Consistent Equations $\det[A] \neq 0$	Inconsistent Equations $\det[A] = 0$	Dependent Equations $\det[A] = 0$
Geometry			
Algebra			
Solution			

Section 8.4 Conic Sections

Preparation   **Objectives**

- Use specific parameters and formulas to find equations for conic sections.

- Identify the standard forms of conic sections centered at the origin.

- Graph conic sections on a calculator, using two functions when required.

- Explore, with a graphing calculator, how changing parameters changes the shape or orientation of the curve.

Links

- Pythagorean theorem: Section 3.1.
- Parabola: Section 3.2.
- Inverse variation: Section 5.2.
- Hyperbola: Section 5.2.
- Distance formula: Section 6.3.
- Conic section equations: Section 8.5.

Time and Emphasis

50 minutes. Optional material.

Vocabulary

| axis | circle | conic section | conical surface |
| hyperbola | parabola | radius | rectangular hyperbola |

Points to Stress

- We find intercepts by substituting $x = 0$ or $y = 0$ in an equation.
- To identify a conic section from its equation, arrange the equation in standard form. Note: See the table on page 607 for a summary of distinguishing features.

Suggested Lesson Format

Warm-up: 5 minutes

Questions on Homework: 10 minutes

Lecture/Group Activity: 25 minutes

Coaching for Homework: 5 minutes

Materials Needed for Class

If available, a commercially produced clear plastic or wood model of the conical surface and various conic sections. (If necessary, make your own with a pair of Styrofoam cones available in craft stores.)

Optional Activity

Take a flashlight into class, shut down the lights, and demonstrate the conic sections with the cone of light. Holding the flashlight perpendicular to the wall gives a circle, tilting the flashlight slightly off perpendicular gives an ellipse, holding the flashlight at a sharp angle relative to the wall gives a parabola, and holding the flashlight parallel to the wall gives one branch of a hyperbola.

Homework

Core exercises: 3 to 19, odd; 23 to 43, odd.

Sample assignment: 1 to 43, odd, 49.

> **NOTE**
> It is recommended that this section be used to review the following topics at the end of the course:
> - Applications with the Pythagorean theorem.
> - Solving second degree equations for a variable, plotting points and drawing graphs.
> - Finding intercepts from a given equation (let x = 0 or let y = 0).
>
> Keep a review focus and an overview or introduction to the conics rather than presenting an in-depth emphasis on memorizing types of equations and detailed vocabulary (such as directrix, foci, and asymptotes which were intentionally omitted from the text material).

For Labs and Recitations

Focus on the shifted circle equation and the graphing calculator by doing the project in Exercise 53.

In Class

Warm-up

(5 minutes): Have the students work in groups on the Warm-up.

Questions on Homework

(10 minutes): Have the students go over the homework in groups and select questions for class discussion.

Lecture/Group Activity

(25 minutes): Comment to the class that the Warm-up reminds us of the Pythagorean theorem and the distance formula.

Conic sections. Introduce the conical surface and show how slicing it gives some possibly familiar (parabola and circle) and unfamiliar (ellipse and hyperbola) shapes.

Circles and ellipses. Develop the equation of a circle using the Pythagorean theorem shown in Example 1.

Have the students do Example 3, making sketches of circles and ellipses using intercepts.

Give the standard equation of an ellipse.

Hyperbola. When we change the addition to a subtraction in the ellipse formula we obtain a hyperbola. First find the intercepts and then solve the equations for y and graph on a calculator. Have the students do Example 6 to practice using the intercepts to check that their graphs are correct.

Parabola. Remind the students that we studied parabolas in Chapters 3 and 4 in quadratic equations. The graphs of quadratic functions are parabolas but not all parabolas are quadratic functions. Have the students graph $y = x^2$ and $x = y^2$.

Discuss the summary box on page 607.

Coaching for Homework

(5 minutes): *Exercises 3 to 20 focus on writing equations from information.*

Exercises 23 to 44 focus on identifying the conic section from its equation.

Exercises 49 to 52 return to setting up systems of equations and using matrices to solve for variables. Remember, each ordered pair identifies what to substitute for x and y in the given equation to obtain one equation in D, E, and F.

Section 8.5 Solving Nonlinear Systems of Equations by Substitution and Graphing

Preparation

Objectives
- Predict the number of solutions to a system including nonlinear equations by identifying the conic sections within the system.
- Solve systems including nonlinear equations with a calculator.
- Solve systems algebraically by substitution.

Links
- Substitution: Section 8.0
- Graphing: Section 8.1.
- Conic sections: Section 8.4.
- Exponential and logarithmic equations: Sections 7.1 and 7.3.

Time and Emphasis
50 minutes. Optional material.

Vocabulary
nonlinear system

Points to Stress
- Sketching graphs of nonlinear systems helps us predict the number of solutions.

Suggested Lesson Format
Warm-up: 5 minutes

Questions on Homework: 10 minutes

Lecture/Group Activity: 25 minutes

Coaching for Homework: 5 minutes

Materials Needed for Class
None

Homework
Core exercises: 1 to 17, every other odd; 25 to 31, odd.

Sample assignment: 1 to 31, odd.

Note: Exercises 1 to 24 focus on linear equations and conic sections. Exercises 25 to 41 focus on exponential and logarithmic equations.

For Labs and Recitations
Example 8 returns to changing exponent expressions and thus reviews properties of exponents. Discuss the example, which properties it uses, and practice with Exercises 33 to 40.

In Class

Warm-up

(5 minutes): Have the students work in pairs on the Warm-up.

Questions on Homework

(10 minutes): Have the students go over the homework in groups and select questions for class discussion.

Lecture/Group Activity

(25 minutes): Nonlinear systems including conic sections. Explain to the class that when we solve a system containing conic sections, first we sketch the graphs of the equations and predict the number of solutions.

Have students work in pairs to graph the equations in Example 3 and predict the number of solutions.

Then solve by substitution. Use the graph and substitution to check the solutions.

Nonlinear systems including exponential and logarithmic equations. Have students work in pairs to graph (by calculator) the equations in Example 6, observe the number of intersections and then solve by substitution.

Instruct the students to use the graph and substitution to check the solutions.

Coaching for Homework

(5 minutes): *Be sure to include sketches of graphs with each system in Exercises 1 to 20 and 25 to 32.*

Section 8.6 Solving Systems of Inequalities

Preparation

Objectives
- Identify quadrants described by inequalities.
- Describe quadrants with inequalities.
- Solve systems of linear inequalities.
- Find inequalities for conic sections.
- Solve systems of nonlinear inequalities.

Links
- Logical statements: Section 1.0.
- Quadrants: Section 1.0.
- Inequalities and lines: Section 1.4.
- Quadratic inequalities: Section 3.5.
- Nonlinear equations: Section 8.4.

Time and Emphasis
50 minutes. Optional material.

Vocabulary
logical statement *a* or *b*   logical statement *a* and *b*

Points to Stress
- Solve a system of inequalities by graphing the inequalities separately and then identifying the overlapping region.

Suggested Lesson Format
Warm-up: 5 minutes

Questions on Homework: 10 minutes

Lecture/Group Activity: 25 minutes

Coaching for Homework: 5 minutes

Materials Needed for Class
None

Homework
Core exercises: 1 to 11, odd; 17 to 33, odd.

Sample assignment: 1 to 33, odd.

For Labs and Recitations
Return to Exercises 43 and 44 of Section 8.5 and do the projects in pairs of students.

In Class

Warm-up

(5 minutes): Have the students work in groups on the Warm-up.

Questions on Homework

(10 minutes): Have the students go over the homework in groups and select questions for class discussion.

Lecture/Group Activity

(25 minutes): Introduce the two logical statements *a or b* and *a and b*.

Do Example 1 with the class to show how we identify what quadrants are described by $x > 0$ or $y > 0$.

Do Example 2 with the class to show how we describe the first quadrant and third quadrant in terms of inequalities.

Solving systems of linear inequalities. Explain to the class that there are many applications where the solution is a region rather than a point. Discuss the effective drug range in Figure 37.

Have the students work in groups to graph the inequalities in Example 3.

Discuss the overlap as the region where the first AND the second inequality are true.

Second-degree inequalities. Have the students work in groups to graph the inequalities in Example 4.

Solving systems of non-linear inequalities. Have student groups do Example 6.

Coaching for Homework

(5 minutes): *Review the key features of the conic section equations in the summary table on page 607.*

TIP Graphing Quadrants on a Graphing Calculator

We can use the shading feature built-in to the [y=] to graph the quadrants.

The calculator does not distinguish between $y > 0$ and $y \geq 0$ or between $y < 0$ and $y \leq 0$. You will need to show the difference on your hand-drawn graphs. To graph $y > 0$ or $y < 0$, we enter the equation $y = 0$ and shade above or below it with the shading option to the left of the y in the [y=] display.

In regular function mode the calculator will not graph the vertical lines $x = 0$, $x = 5$, etc. However, we can approximate a vertical line by drawing a line with a very large slope; such as $y = 1000x$. Thus, to graph $x > 0$ or $x < 0$, enter the equation $y = 1000x$ and then shade the appropriate side. To graph $x > 5$ or $x < 5$, enter $y = 1000(x - 5)$ and shade the appropriate side.

Answer Key

to

Section Activities

The FBI's Ten Most Un-Wanted Errors
Review Quiz

1. Simplify and compare: $\sqrt{-4}$ and $-\sqrt{4}$

    $\sqrt{-4}$ **is undefined in the real numbers and** $-\sqrt{4}$ **$= -2$. The first is not a real number.**

2. Subtract: $5 - (-3)$

    8

3. Simplify: $6 - 3(x - 7)$

    27 - 3x or -3x + 27

4. Simplify: $(-4)^2$ and -4^2

    16 and −16

5. Simplify: $(-2)^2$ and $-(-2)^2$

    4 and −4

6. Are $(-x)^2$ and $-x^2$ equal? Explain your answer.

    No, x^2 and $-x^2$ The base in the first is $-x$ and the base in the second is x.

7. Evaluate by hand and then on your calculator: $(8 - \sqrt{(36)} / (3 - 5)$

    11

    There is one parentheses missing. A calculator will assume it is at the end of the expression, after the five and the last parentheses, 5).

8. Evaluate by hand and then on your calculator: $(8 - \sqrt{(36)}) / (3 - 5)$

    -1

9. Compare the results in Questions 7 and 8. How do you explain the difference?

    The parentheses are different in Questions 7 and 8. In Question 7, a calculator will assume a parenthesis belongs at the end of the expression, after the 5. In Question 8, the second parenthesis after 36, outside the square root symbol, creates a single fraction with $8 - \sqrt{(36)}$ in the numerator and $3 - 5$ in the denominator.

10. Simplify $A = 5\{6 - 4[3 - 8(5 - 7) + 1] - 2\}$

    −320

    This is the puzzle problem from Section 1.0, Example 11, which uses the order of operations.

Section 4.1, IRM page 68

Optional Activity Have groups find missing terms on the left of each sequence, then use regression to find the quadratic equation describing each sequence.

1. ___, ___, ___, 1, 4, 9, 16, ...   **4, 1, 0;** $y = x^2$

2. ___, ___, ___, 2, 6, 12, 20, ...   **2, 0, 0;** $y = x^2 + x$

3. ___, ___, ___, 1, 3, 6, 10, 15, ...   **1, 0, 0;** $y = 0.5x^2 + 0.5x$

4. ___, ___, ___, −1, 1, 7, 17, 31, ...   **17, 7, 1;** $y = 2x^2 - 4x + 1$

5. ___, ___, ___, 4, −1, −8, −17, −28, ...   **7, 8, 7;** $y = -1x^2 - 2x + 7$

6. ___, ___, ___, 0, −7, −20, −39, −64, ...   **−15, −4, 1;** $y = -3x^2 + 2x + 1$

Quadratic Function Activity

<u>Materials needed</u>: Graph paper and a graphing calculator.

<u>Activity</u>: The purpose of this activity is to explore quadratic functions. These functions are written in the general form $y = ax^2 + bx + c$, where a, b, and c are constants similar to the constants in the linear function, $y = mx + b$.

Part 1

For each of the graphs below find the following:
   a. The x-intercepts (there could be one, two or none of these).
   b. The y-intercept (there should be only one; why is this?).
   c. The axis of symmetry (on the x-axis).
   d. The ordered pair that describes the vertex. (the highest or lowest point on the graph).
   e. The domain and range of the graph (assume that each graph continues in the direction shown by the arrows on the graph).

1. a. **(1, 0) and (3, 0)**

   b. **(0, –3)**

   c. **$x = 2$**

   d. **(2, 1)**

   e. **all real numbers; (–infinity, 1]**

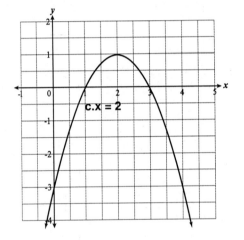

2. a. **None**

   b. **(0, 5)**

   c. **$x = 2$**

   d. **(2, 1)**

   e. **all real numbers; [1, infinity)**

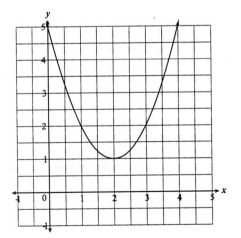

146

3. a. $(-1.6, 0)$ $(-4.4, 0)$

   b. $(0, 7)$

   c. $x = -3$

   d. $(-3, -2)$

   e. **all real numbers; [−2, infinity)**

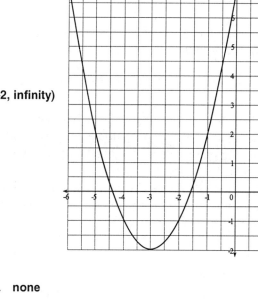

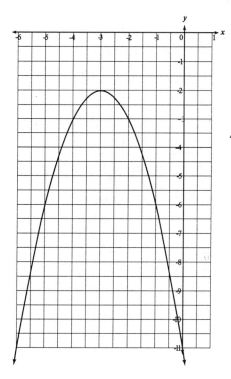

4. a. **none**

   b. $(0, -11)$

   c. $x = -3$

   d. $(-3, -2)$

   e. **all real numbers; (−infinity, −2]**

5. a. $(1, 0)$

   b. $(0, 1)$

   c. $x = 1$

   d. $(1, 0)$

   e. **all real numbers; [0, infinity)**

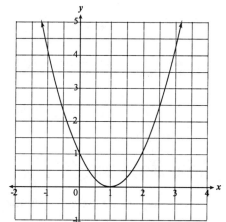

6. Using complete sentences, explain the relationship between the axis of symmetry and the vertex..

The vertex lies on the axis of symmetry. The equation of the axis of symmetry also gives the *x-coordinate* of the vertex.

7. Using complete sentences, explain the relationship between the vertex and the range of each function.

The minimum or maximum finite y-value of the range is the same as the y-value of the vertex.

8. Using complete sentences describe the general shape of the graphs. (Are these functions? What is this shape called?)

       All graphs in 1 to 5 are functions and symmetric (parabolic) in shape.

Part 2

For each of the equations below, identify the values a, b, and c.

1. $f(x) = -x^2 + 4x - 3$ **$a = -1$ $b = 4$ $c = -3$**

2. $f(x) = (x - 2)^2 + 1$ **$a = 1$ $b = -4$ $c = 5$**

3. $f(x) = x^2 + 6x + 7$ **$a = 1$ $b = 6$ $c = 7$**

4. $f(x) = -x^2 - 6x - 11$ **$a = -1$ $b = -6$ $c = -11$**

5. $f(x) = (x - 1)^2$ **$a = 1$ $b = -2$ $c = 1$**

     a. If you graph each of the functions above, which graphs will open up? **2, 3, and 5**

     b. If you graph each of the functions above, which graphs will open down? **1 and 4**

6. The functions listed in Part 2 match the graphs in Part 1. How does the value of a impact each graph? (If you are unsure try graphing $y = x^2$ and $y = -x^2$. What do you notice?)

The constant *a* determines whether the parabola opens up or down: If *a* > 0, the parabola opens up; if *a* < 0, the parabola opens down.

7. Compare the y-intercept of each graph in Part 1 with the functions listed in Part 2. How does the value of c impact each graph?

The value of *c* is the *y-coordinate* of the y-intercept.

Part 3

Let's investigate *a* more closely. Graph the following functions on the same axes.

1. $f(x) = x^2$

2. $f(x) = 2x^2$

3. $f(x) = -2x^2$

4. $f(x) = 0.5x^2$

5. $f(x) = 0.1x^2$

6. $f(x) = 4x^2$

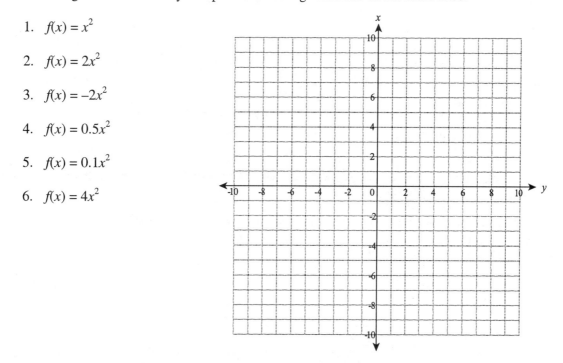

7. Given what you have just graphed, how would you modify your answer to Exercise 6 in Part 2? Carefully explain the impact the constant *a* will have on any quadratic graph using as much detail as necessary.

   In addition to negative and positive values of *a*, if |*a*| > 1, then the parabola is steep, and if |*a*| < 1, then the parabola is less steep.

8. Without actually graphing the function describe what the graph will look like for the following function (be sure to describe it so that someone without a calculator would know how to draw it!): $f(x) = -0.3x^2 + 6$.

   The parabola opens downwards and is not very steep. It is shifted vertically 6 units up the y-axis.

Section 4.4, pages 81 to 83

Shifty Functions

The general form for a quadratic function is $f(x) = ax^2 + bx + c$. Another way to write a quadratic function is $y = (x - h)^2 + k$ or if we move k to the left side, we get $y - k = (x - h)^2$. To derive this new form of a quadratic function, we would use the completing the square method. We will not focus on arriving at this form. Rather, we will focus on what the constants h and k tell us about the graph.

1. Identify h and k in the following functions:

   b. $y = (x - 2)^2 - 4$ b. $y = (x + 3)^2 - 1$ c. $y - 5 = (x + 4)^2$ d. $y + 2 = (x - 3)^2$

   $h = 2, \ k = -4$ **$h = -3, \ k = -1$**   **$h = -4, \ k = 5$**   **$h = 3, \ k = -2$**

Have the instructor check your work before moving on to Exercise 2.

2. Use your calculator to graph each of the functions in Exercise 1. Be sure to change Parts c and d to the form $y = (x - h)^2 + k$ by moving the k to the right side of the equation. Make sketches of the graphs below.

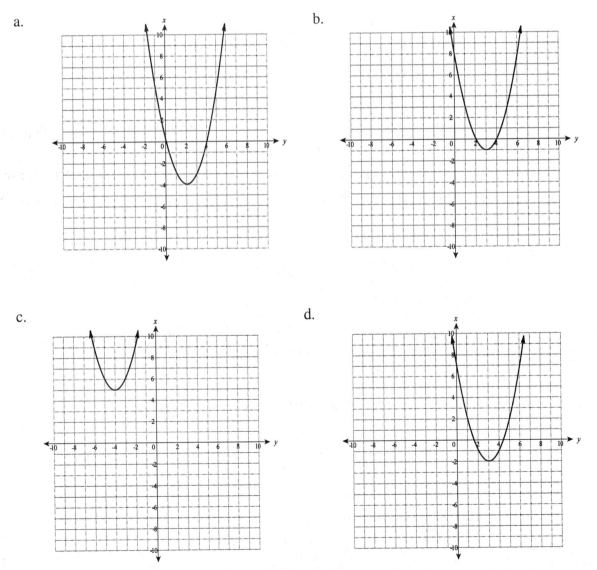

a.

b.

c.

d.

3. For each of the graphs in Exercise 2, identify the vertex.

   a.   **(2 , –4)**   b. **(–3 , –1)**   c. **(–4 , 5)**   d. **(3 , –2)**

4. With your calculator set at the standard screen size, graph each of the following
   functions together. (Remember the order in which they are being graphed.) Make
   sketches of the graphs on the same axes. <u>Label each function</u>.
   a. $y = x^2$ b. $y = x^2 + 4$ c. $y = x^2 - 8$ d. $y = x^2 - 2$

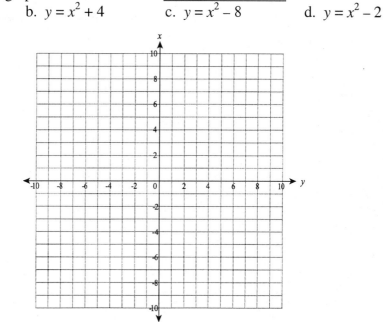

5. In a complete sentence or two, describe what effect k has on the graph. Notice that all of
   the functions in Exercise 4 are written in the form $y = (x - 0)^2 + k$.

   k shifts the graph vertically k spaces. If $k > 0$, the graph moves up. If $k < 0$, the graph shifts down.

6. On a new screen, graph all of the following functions. Make sketches of the graphs on
   the same axes. Label the axes. <u>Label the functions.</u>
   a. $y = x^2$ b. $y = (x - 2)^2$ c. $y = (x + 7)^2$ d. $y = (x + 4)^2$

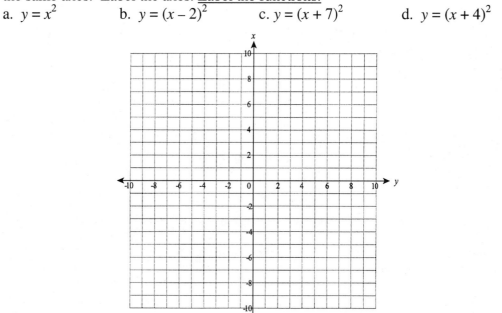

7. In a complete sentence or two, describe the effect that h has on the graph. Notice that all of the functions in Exercise 6 were written in the form $y - 0 = (x - h)^2$ or $y = (x - h)^2 + 0$.

h shifts the graph horizontally h units along the x-axis. If $h > 0$ the shift is to the right, if $h < 0$ the shift is to the left. Note: Many students will state this just the opposite since they do not distinguish $x - h$ from $x + h$. This is a good time to remind the students that $-h$ could be a positive number!

8. Before using your calculator, make educated guesses about the shapes of these graphs. Identify h and k. Check your guesses on the calculator. (You may have to move k to the right side of the equation.) Sketch each graph on the same axes.

   b. $y = (x - 3)^2 + 6$
      $h = 3$ $k = 6$

   c. $y + 3 = (x - 6)^2$
      $h = 6$ $k = -3$

   b. $y = (x + 5)^2 - 4$
      $h = -5$ $k = -4$

   d. $y - 6 = (x + 7)^2$
      $h = -7$ $k = 6$

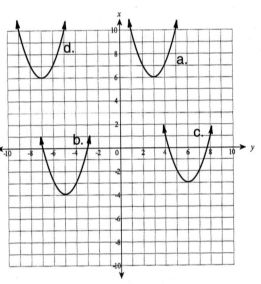

9. Identify the vertex in each of the parabolas in Exercise 8. In a sentence or two, explain how h and k relate to the vertex?

   a. **vertex = (3, 6)**

   c. **vertex = (6, –3)**

   b. **vertex = (–5, –4)**

   d. **vertex = (–7, 6)**

   h shifts the vertex from $x = 0$ to $x = h$. k shifts the vertex from $y = 0$ to $y = k$, so the vertex is (h, k).

10. Graph $y = (x - 2)^2 + 6$ on your calculator. Notice what happens to the vertex if you change the value of a in $y = a(x - h)^2 + k$. Graph the following.

   a. $y = 3(x - 2)^2 + 6$ b. $y = -3(x - 2)^2 + 6$ c. $y = 0.3(x - 2)^2 + 6$

Write a sentence describing what impact a has on the vertex of a parabola?

The coefficient, a, has no impact on the placement of the vertex of a parabola. It makes the parabola more or less steep and makes the parabola open up.

Not-So-Simple Fractions

1. Find the value(s) of x for which the following expressions are undefined:

a. $\dfrac{2x-1}{3-x}$

b. $\dfrac{2x-1}{3x}$

c. $\dfrac{2x-1}{x^2-7x+10}$

$x = 3$

$x = 0$

$x = 2$ or $x = 5$

2. Simplify the expressions:

a. $\dfrac{4x}{6y}$

b. $\dfrac{3x(x+2)}{6xy}$

c. $\dfrac{xy+y^2}{xy}$

$\dfrac{2x}{3y}$

$\dfrac{x+2}{2y}$

$\dfrac{y}{1} = y$

3. The additive inverse of an expression is achieved by taking the opposite sign of the expression. For example, the additive inverse of 2 is –2. The additive inverse of $-x$ is x. The additive inverse of $1 - x$ is $-1 + x$. Find the additive inverses of the following expressions.

a. $1 + a$

b. $3 - 5x$

c. $x - 7y$

$-1 - a$

$-3 + 5x$

$-x + 7y$

Simplifying Complex Fractions

Start here:

The following set of expressions form a closed system under the operation of substitution (known in higher courses as composition of functions).

$$A: \frac{1}{1-x}; \quad B: \frac{x-1}{x}$$

$$C: \frac{x}{x-1}; \quad D: \frac{1}{x}$$

$$E: 1-x; \quad F: x$$

Example substitutions:

A into A gives $\dfrac{1}{1-\left(\dfrac{1}{1-x}\right)}$ and simplifies to $\dfrac{x-1}{x}$ or B.

Do the simplification by hand to check the result.

A into B gives $\dfrac{\left(\dfrac{1}{1-x}\right)-1}{\left(\dfrac{1}{1-x}\right)}$ and simplifies to x, or F.

Do the simplification by hand to check the result.

The results for A into A and A into B are shown in the table below.

Within your group, complete the table for the expressions A, B, and F.

	A	B	F
A	B	F	A
B	F	A	B
F	A	B	F

Extensions:

1. Identities.

   When we multiply 1 times an expression, *n*, the answer is *n*. We say 1 is the multiplicative identity.
   When we add 0 to an expression, *n*, the answer is *n*. We say 0 is the *additive identity*.
   When we substitute **x** in each expression, *n*, the answer is *n*. We say expression **x** is the *substitution identity*.

2. Inverses.

   When we multiply a number by its reciprocal (or *multiplicative inverse*), we get 1, the multiplicative identity.
   When we add a number to its opposite (or *additive inverse*), we get 0, the additive identity.
   When we substitute **A** into **B** and **B** into **A** we get *x*, the substitution identity.
   The two expressions, **A** and **B** are called inverses.

3. An extended project.

   To complete the full table for all six expressions, there are 36 different substitutions to perform: each of *A*, *B*, *C*, *D*, *E*, and *F* (on the left side of the table) is substituted into each expression (listed across the top of the table).

	A	B	C	D	E	F
A	B	F	D	E	C	A
B	F	A	E	C	D	B
C	E	D	F	B	A	C
D	C	E	A	F	B	D
E	D	C	B	A	F	E
F	A	B	C	D	E	F

4. Does *F* continue to be the identity in the full table? **yes**

5. *A* into *B* and *B* into *A* gave the identity *x* (expression *F*). *A* and *B* are inverses. Is there another pair of expressions like *A* and *B* that when substituted into each other give *x*, the identity? **no**

6. Which expressions give *x* when substituted into themselves?
   C is its own inverse as are D, E, and F their own inverses.